Great Meals in Minutes was created by
Rebus, Inc.
and published by Time-Life Books.

Rebus, Inc.

Publisher: Rodney Friedman
Editor: Shirley Tomkievicz
Executive Editor: Elizabeth P. Rice
Art Director: Ronald Gross
Managing Editor: Brenda Goldberg
Senior Editor: Cara De Silva
Food Editor and Food Stylist: Grace Young
Photographer: Steven Mays
Prop Stylist: Cathryn Schwing
Staff Writer: Alexandra Greeley
Associate Editor: Jordan Verner
Editorial Assistants: Bonnie J. Slotnick,
Joan Michel
Assistant Food Stylist: Nancy Leland
Thompson
Recipe Tester: Gina Palombi Barclay

For information about any Time-Life book,
please write:
Reader Information
Time-Life Books
541 North Fairbanks Court
Chicago, Illinois 60611

Library of Congress Cataloging in Publication Data
Beef and veal menus.
    (Great meals in minutes)
    Includes index.
    1. Cookery (Beef)   2. Cookery (Veal)   3. Menus.
    4. Cooks—United States—Biography.
I. Time-Life Books.   II. Series.
TX749.B386   1984   642   83-24175
ISBN 0-86706-174-X (retail ed.)
ISBN 0-86706-175-8 (lib. bdg.)

Time-Life Books Inc.
is a wholly owned subsidiary of

Time Incorporated

Founder: Henry R. Luce 1898–1967
Editor-in-Chief: Henry Anatole Grunwald
President: J. Richard Munro
Chairman of the Board: Ralph P. Davidson
Corporate Editor: Jason McManus
Group Vice President, Books: Joan D. Manley

Time-Life Books Inc.

Editor: George Constable
Executive Editor: George Daniels
Director of Design: Louis Klein
Board of Editors: Dale M. Brown, Thomas
A. Lewis, Robert G. Mason, Ellen Phillips,
Peter Pocock, Gerry Schremp, Gerald
Simons, Rosalind Stubenberg, Kit van
Tulleken, Henry Woodhead
Director of Administration: David L. Harrison
Director of Research: Carolyn L. Sackett
Director of Photography: John Conrad Weiser

President: Reginald K. Brack Jr.
Senior Vice President: William Henry
Vice Presidents: George Artandi, Stephen L.
Bair, Robert A. Ellis, Juanita T. James,
Christopher T. Linen, James L. Mercer,
Joanne A. Pello, Paul R. Stewart

Editorial Operations
Design: Anne B. Landry (art coordinator);
James J. Cox (quality control)
Research: Phyllis K. Wise (assistant director),
Louise D. Forstall
Copy Room: Diane Ullius
Production: Celia Beattie, Gordon E. Buck
Correspondent: Miriam Hsia (New York)

SERIES CONSULTANT
Margaret E. Happel is the author of *Ladies
Home Journal Adventures in Cooking,
Ladies Home Journal Handbook of Holiday
Cuisine,* and other best-selling cookbooks, as
well as the translator and adapter of Rebecca
Hsu Hiu Min's *Delights of Chinese Cooking.*
A food consultant based in New York City,
she has been director of the food department
of *Good Housekeeping* and editor of
American Home magazine.

WINE CONSULTANT
Tom Maresca combines a full-time career
teaching English literature with writing
about and consuming fine wines. He is now
at work on *The Wine Case Book,* which
explains the techniques of wine tasting.

Cover: Victoria Wise's warm tarragon-
mushroom salad, beef roulade, and cottage
fried potatoes. See pages 86–87.

Great Meals
IN MINUTES

BEEF & VEAL
MENUS

TIME
LIFE
BOOKS

TIME-LIFE BOOKS, ALEXANDRIA, VIRGINIA

Contents

Meet the Cooks

STEVIE BASS

Born and raised in Connecticut, Stevie Bass studied food, nutrition, art, and design in college and used this training for her career in recipe development and food styling. Now living in San Francisco, she runs her own consulting firm, Food Concepts, which works with advertising and public relations agencies, photographers, filmmakers, and food companies in the San Francisco area.

JIM FOBEL

Jim Fobel is the author of *Beautiful Food*, *The Big Book of Fabulous Fun-Filled Celebrations and Holiday Crafts*, and *The Stencil Book*. A former test-kitchen director for *Food & Wine* magazine, he writes about food for many national publications. He is the founder of the Picture Pie Company, Stencil-Magic, and The Whole Kit and Kaboodle Company. A graduate of the Otis Art Institute in California, Jim Fobel now lives and works in New York City.

DIANA STURGIS

Welsh by birth and now living in Brooklyn with her family, Diana Sturgis graduated from the University of Wales in Cardiff with a teaching diploma. She taught cooking and nutrition in school and at college for eight years before moving to the United States. Her background includes work as a recipe developer and tester for a New York food company and as a freelance food stylist. At present, she is director of the test kitchen for *Food & Wine* magazine.

NORMAN WEINSTEIN

Norman Weinstein, a native New Yorker with a Master's degree in music and a love of Chinese food and cooking, founded The Hot Wok, a cooking school and catering business in Brooklyn. He has written two books on Chinese cooking, including *Chinese Cooking: The Classical Techniques Made Easy*, and is the editor of *Wok Talk*, a newsletter about Chinese cooking. An instructor at the New York Cooking Center, he was the founder of the New York Association of Cooking Teachers.

VICTORIA FAHEY

Victoria Fahey, a self-taught cook, is a partner in The Food Company, a specialty food store, café, and catering company in Gualala, California. She was previously associated with Curds & Whey in Oakland and has contributed recipes to the *California Seafood Cookbook* and *Bon Appétit Appetizers*.

JACK UBALDI

Born in Perugia, Italy, master butcher Jack Ubaldi moved to New York as a young boy. For several decades he was both owner and butcher of the Florence Meat Market in Manhattan. After he retired, he launched the Culinary Arts Program at the New School for Social Research and he now teaches three different courses, the most comprehensive being the professional butchering classes at the New York Restaurant School.

MARY BETH CLARK

Mary Beth Clark—chef, teacher, researcher, and consultant—is founder of the Manhattan cooking school that bears her name and of The Food Consulting Group, a research/consulting firm for the food, wine, and cookware industries. She developed the first cooking course in America to cover all seven regions of China and has devised both salt-free Chinese and American recipes and allergy-sensitive recipes, which have appeared in newspapers and magazines.

VICTORIA WISE

Victoria Wise, a self-taught cook, has been cooking professionally since 1971, when she left her graduate studies in philosophy to become the first chef at Berkeley's Chez Panisse, a restaurant well known to U.S. gastronomes. She left Chez Panisse in 1973 to start her own charcuterie, a Pig by the Tail Charcuterie, in Berkeley, California.

GENE HOVIS

Gene Hovis, a native of North Carolina, has been involved in the food business in New York for over 25 years, working as a caterer, restaurant consultant, professional chef, and food stylist. Currently executive chef of a New York textile firm's corporate dining rooms, he also acts as a consultant on projects such as the biannual Anuga Food Show in Cologne, Germany, and has just completed his first cookbook, a collection of Southern family recipes.

Beef & Veal Menus in Minutes

GREAT MEALS FOR FOUR, IN AN HOUR OR LESS

Accoording to *Larousse Gastronomique*, the most famous of all culinary encyclopedias, "Beef is the best, most fortifying and most nourishing of all butcher's meat." American meat eaters would certainly add that beef (the meat of fully grown cattle) and veal (the meat of newborn to three-month-old calves) are appetizing.

Both beef and veal are highly nutritious. They contain high-quality protein and are a complete source of the essential amino acids. Beef is an excellent source of B vitamins, particularly B–12, and iron, and contributes substantial amounts of phosphorous and zinc to the human diet. Furthermore, recent findings indicate that, if eaten in moderation, beef and veal do not pose a problem with cholesterol.

No wonder that Americans have become a nation of confirmed beef eaters. But this has not always been the case. Despite America's "red meat" image—so popular with foreigners—the beef industry did not boom until after World War II, when an increasingly affluent American public could afford to buy beef regularly. In the mid-1950s, retail beef sales finally outstripped pork sales, making beef the best seller. Today, Americans still eat more beef than any other meat, including chicken.

United States Department of Agriculture (USDA) data indicate that the finest year for beef sales was 1976, when consumers purchased 94.4 pounds retail weight of beef per person. More recent figures show that this peak has dipped recently to 77.3 pounds of beef per person, still a remarkable annual total of 18 billion pounds of beef purchased. However, veal has never captured more than a fraction of the meat-eating market, largely because United States cattle-farmers find raising calves to maturity more economical than slaughtering them at three months. Therefore, veal has never enjoyed equal billing on the American table due to both its relative rarity and higher price. Europeans, on the other hand, lack adequate pasturage for large beef herds, so that veal is readily obtainable in markets.

Nevertheless, making beef generally available was a

Two veal rib chops with scallions, and a shell steak with mushrooms, fresh sage, and garlic, opposite, are components of satisfying meals. On the tabletop and on the cutting board are a few of the seasonings and fresh vegetables that enhance both veal and beef (clockwise, from top left): whole lemons, red bell pepper, decanters of herb-flavored oil and of vinegar, red onion, shallots, garlic cloves, and a bunch of fresh thyme.

slow process: cattle have a long history. The wild ox *(Bos primogenitus)*, the forebear of modern cattle, was first domesticated between 10,000 and 6000 B.C. in Turkey and Greece. For millenia thereafter, people used it for work rather than for food. As agrarian communities flourished, however, the ox turned up more often in the cookpot: ancient Egyptians raised a sturdy longhorn for meat; the Greeks often served seasoned boiled beef on their banquet tables; and the Chinese listed ox ribs as one of their kitchen triumphs. Apicius, a Roman cookbook author of the first century A.D., described various spiced-beef recipes.

Today, several hundred breeds of cattle are scattered throughout the world. This diverse genetic pool allows cattle-farmers to select their herds for climate, disease resistance, and type of grazing land. Many breeds are raised specifically for their meat, while others are selected as dairy stock. Several countries are major producers of beef cattle, including Brazil, Argentina, Uruguay, Australia, and Mexico—and the world's top-ranking producer, the United States. Japan produces limited supplies of the highly prized, famous Kobe beef. These pampered steers are raised by hand, fed beer, and curried and massaged daily to disperse fat throughout the muscle, producing a well-marbled meat. This beef, experts claim, ranks among the world's tenderest.

Most American beef cattle are descendants of the English stock imported by early colonists. During America's early history, while wild game was still plentiful, cattle were valued mainly for their hides, dairy products, and draft labor. Even so, the first American cookbook, written by Amelia Simmons in 1796, discussed the relative cooking qualities of ox beef versus cow beef. Furthermore, she instructed her readers to roast beef over a brisk fire, time the cooking according to the tenderness of the beef, and, that beef "rare done is the healthiest and the taste of this age." Tips such as these, by helping to produce better meals, gradually increased the popularity of beef.

Americans slowly developed an appetite for beef. By the 1860s, with the advent of railroads that permitted shipping beef from grazing lands to Eastern markets, beef production and supplies had expanded. During the following decades, massive cattle drives from the Southwest to Midwest railheads made fresh beef available nationwide. The later development of refrigeration clinched a permanent place for beef in the American diet.

Today the beef industry, although further refined, oper-

Cooking at high temperatures can be dangerous, but not if you follow a few simple tips:

▶ Water added to hot fat will always cause spattering. If possible, pat foods dry with a cloth or paper towel before you add them to the hot oil in a skillet, Dutch oven, or wok.

▶ Lay the food in the pan gently. Otherwise the fat will certainly spatter.

▶ Be aware of your cooking environment. If you are boiling or steaming some foods while sautéing others, place the pots far enough apart so the water is unlikely to splash into the oil.

▶ Turn pot handles inward, toward the middle of the stove, so that you do not accidentally knock something over.

▶ Remember that alcohol—wine, brandy, or spirits—may occasionally catch fire when you add it to a very hot pan. If this happens, stand back for your own protection, and then quickly cover the pan with a lid. The fire will instantly subside, and the food will be just as good as ever.

▶ Keep pot holders and mitts close enough to be handy, but never hang them above the burners; nor should you lay them on the stove top.

---

ates much as it did during the nineteenth century. Cattle—primarily steers and heifers not used for breeding—are raised on the open range. They are then shipped to feedlots for further growth on a more controlled diet, and are fed flavor-giving grains such as corn, soybeans, barley, and sorghum. The major recent change in the beef industry has come through improved selection of superior bulls and cows for special breeding programs. This selective breeding has enabled American cattle-farmers to produce quality beef systematically, and should, in time, help to produce quality beef worldwide.

Retail cuts of beef and veal, wisely selected and carefully prepared, provide an endless source of superb meals. You need master only a handful of basic skills to produce these meals.

On the following pages, nine of America's most talented cooks present 28 complete menus featuring beef and veal. Every menu can be made in an hour or less, and the cooks focus on a new kind of American cuisine that borrows ideas and techniques from around the world but also values American native traditions. They use fresh produce, with no powdered sauces or other dubious shortcuts. The other ingredients (vinegars, spices, herbs, and so on) are all high quality yet available for the most part in supermarkets or, occasionally, in a specialty shop. Each of the menus serves four people and includes other dishes that work perfectly with beef or veal.

The photographs accompanying each meal show exactly how the dishes will look when you bring them to the table. The cooks and the test kitchen have planned the meals for appearance as well as taste: the vegetables are brilliant and fresh, the visual combinations appetizing. The table settings feature bright colors, simple flower arrangements, and attractive, but not necessarily expensive, serving pieces. You can readily adapt your own tableware to these menus in convenient ways that will please you and your guests.

For each menu, the Editors, with advice from the cooks, suggest wine and other beverages. And there are suggestions for the best uses of leftovers and for appropriate desserts. On each menu page, too, you will find a range of other tips, from the fastest way to skin a tomato to tricks

for selecting the freshest produce. All the recipes have been tested meticulously to make sure that even a relatively inexperienced cook can complete them within the time limit.

BEFORE YOU START

Great Meals in Minutes is designed for efficiency and ease. The books will work best for you when you follow these suggestions:

1. Read the guidelines (pages 8–11) for selecting the cuts of beef and veal appropriate for quick cooking and suited to the recipe.

2. Refresh your memory on the few simple cooking techniques on the following pages. They will quickly become second nature and will help you produce professional meals in minutes.

3. Read the menus *before* you shop. Each one opens with a list of all the required ingredients, listed in the order you would expect to shop for them in the average supermarket. Check for those few you need to buy; many items will already be on your pantry shelf.

4. Check the equipment list on page 16. A good sharp knife or knives and pots and pans of the right shape and material are essential for making great meals in minutes. This may be the time to look critically at what you own and to plan to buy a few things. The right equipment can turn cooking from a necessity into a creative experience.

5. Get out everything you need before you start to cook: the lists at the beginning of each menu tell just what is required. To save effort, keep your ingredients close at hand and always put them in the same place so you can reach for them instinctively.

6. Take your meat and dairy products from the refrigerator early enough for them to come to room temperature and therefore cut cooking time.

7. Follow the step-by-step game plan with each menu. That way, you can be sure of having the entire meal ready to serve at the right moment.

SELECTING THE RIGHT GRADE OF BEEF AND VEAL

To buy the best meat for a particular dish, the consumer must choose the meat both by the correct grade and the correct cut. For great meals, the meat must be suitable for a specific cooking method and recipe. However, this does not necessitate buying the best grade and cuts, although it is important to learn about the grading, cutting, and labeling system.

Official Inspection
The federal government has set several standards that assure the production and sale of wholesome meat. The Federal Meat Inspection Act of 1906 requires that all meat shipped interstate and sold wholesale in the United States be federally inspected for wholesomeness and cleanness, then stamped with a round seal, "U.S. Inspected and Passed." This stamp guarantees the consumer that the meat comes from healthy animals slaughtered and processed under sanitary conditions. The Wholesome Meat Act of 1967 requires that meat produced and sold wholesale intrastate also must be inspected according to USDA standards. All meat offered for wholesale, therefore, has been stamped with an inspection mark, although this mark may not be visible on retail cuts like steaks.

The Meat Grading System
In 1927, the USDA established a federal grading system, a uniform method for appraising the quality of inspected meat. Not all meat is graded to USDA standards, as meat grading is voluntary; however, in general, the consumer's best bet for quality is to buy USDA graded meat. Alternatively, some retail chains of supermarkets opt to use their own grading systems and standards, and in this case, retailers should provide an explanation of their own special system.

Meat grading indicates palatability, that is, tenderness, juiciness, and flavor, and the grades are set in part by these two criteria: *marbling* and *color*.

Marbling is the amount of interior fat that interlaces the meat, one of the most important factors affecting tenderness, taste, and juiciness. Prime beef is well-marbled, with parallel flecks of fat resembling paint splatters; choice beef has thinner and sparser marbling; and the good grade has almost no marbling. Since veal comes from young animals, it has little, if any, marbling from stored fat.

Fresh beef typically has bright red meat with firm ivory-colored fat. Good veal has light pinkish-white meat, and the small amount of external fat is also ivory-colored.

Of the eight official beef grades, only the highest three are generally available in retail markets. The other grades are usually reserved for ground beef products or processed meats. Of the six veal grades, only the two best grades, Prime and Choice, are available to consumers.

Prime: Because USDA prime beef is the highest quality and most expensive, it is produced in limited quantities. Prime beef is sold in many butcher's shops and some supermarkets. Richly marbled throughout, prime beef is the tenderest and most flavorful of all. Prime veal is most readily available to consumers. The meat should be a light pinkish-white color with a soft, smooth, velvety texture, and feel firm to the touch. Prime veal is tender because it comes from young animals, although it lacks marbling.

Choice: USDA choice beef is the most popular grade, and is readily available in most retail meat stores and supermarkets. Less marbled than prime and slightly less flavorful, most choice beef contains enough fat to cook by dry heat and still be tender, though some choice grade cuts require moist-heat cooking. Choice veal may be colored a darker reddish pink, and have a coarser texture, a sign of larger animals and lower quality.

Good: USDA good beef contains less marbling, and is often sold under a house brand name or as economy meat. Although it is as nutritious as the higher grades, beef stamped "good" is lean, so that while some cuts are cooked by dry heat, most cuts require moist-heat cooking to become tender.

Aging
Aged beef, that is, beef stored in a humidity- and temperature-controlled environment for two to six weeks, undergoes natural tenderizing because meat enzymes break down tough fibers. Prime and choice beef are the two grades most commonly aged, and this meat is usually sold to the restaurant trade. However, during shipping and handling, which takes roughly 10 days, all beef ages slightly, except for Kosher beef. Traditional Jewish laws dictate that all meat must be consumed within 72 hours of slaughter, unless specially treated and then frozen. Veal is not aged, as it is already tender.

SELECTING THE RIGHT CUT
Grading helps the consumer select the correct quality meat. But, understanding the anatomy of both beef and veal is the consumer's best guide: *The origin of a cut is the key to tenderness.*

Most meat is muscle, and heavily exercised muscles—the muscles of locomotion—are tougher than rarely used ones (the muscles of suspension). For instance, rib and loin cuts are the tenderest because they lie along the backbone and are the lesser used set of muscles. Frequently used muscles, for example the ones in the shoulder, leg, and neck, are tougher. A prime blade roast from the shoulder will have more fat than a choice sirloin, but because the sirloin comes from the lesser exercised back muscle, the sirloin will be a tenderer cut.

A knowledge of the source of cuts suggests appropriate cooking methods. Less tender cuts have a higher concentration of connective tissue. Cuts such as these, from the leg, neck, and shoulders, require long cooking at low temperatures—braising, poaching, or stewing—to break down the connective tissue and to keep the meat moist and to tenderize it. Tender ribs and loin require only brief cooking—roasting, broiling, pan broiling, grilling, or frying—just long enough to seal in juices and sharpen flavor. Some moderately tender shoulder and rump cuts can be either roasted or moist cooked.

Cooking veal follows a slightly different format. Since it comes from young animals, all veal is relatively tender. However, it has little marbling and therefore, to impart flavor, veal steaks, cutlets, scallops, and chops should be sautéed or braised rather than broiled. Tougher cuts from

CUTS OF MEAT

BEEF

Chuck
Cut from the shoulder portion of the carcass, consisting of the neck, blade, arm, and shoulder. Much of this meat is tough and tastes best when stewed or braised.

Boneless shoulder (clod) steak: A boneless, first cut steak from chuck. Sometimes known as BONELESS BEEF CHUCK SHOULDER STEAK.

Chuck steak: Cut from arm or blade portion of chuck. It may be tough and require stewing or braising to tenderize it.

Rib
Cut from the forequarter of the carcass, directly behind the shoulder, lying along the backbone. The standing rib cut comes from this section, which is tender enough to be roasted.

Rib steak: An inch-thick bone-in steak, cut from the rib roast.

Entrecôte: An inch-thick steak, cut from between the bones of rib roast. Sometimes known as BONELESS BEEF RIB EYE STEAK.

Beef back ribs: Long rib bones directly beneath the rib eye muscle.

Loin
Cut from the mid-portion of the carcass, just in front of the hips, lying along the backbone. The most tender cuts of beef are from this section.

Shell steak: Cut from a bone-in top loin, it has some external fat covering and is very tender. Sometimes known as STRIP STEAKS OR BEEF LOIN TOP LOIN STEAK.

Filet mignon: A 1- to 2-inch-thick steak cut from the tenderloin. Sometimes known as BEEF LOIN TENDERLOIN STEAK.

Tournedos: 1- to 1½-inch-thick slices from the filet mignon portion cut nearest to the center of the tenderloin. Tournedos are exceptionally tender cuts, with little covering fat. Sometimes known as BEEF LOIN, FILET MIGNON, OR BEEF TENDERLOIN STEAK.

Chateaubriand: The thick tender cuts from the central portion of the tenderloin. Sometimes known as BEEF LOIN TENDERLOIN ROAST.

Sirloin steak: Cut from the sirloin section and may have bone in or out. Sometimes known as BEEF LOIN SIRLOIN STEAK.

Top sirloin steak: Sirloin steak with bones and tenderloin removed. Sometimes known as BONELESS BEEF LOIN TOP SIRLOIN STEAK.

Round
Cut from the rump and hind leg of the carcass, it is divided into roasts, steaks, and other tougher cuts.

Round steak: Cut from the leg, either top or bottom. Top round is generally more tender.

Flank
Cut from the belly portion of the underside, it is boneless and lean, but relatively tough.

Flank steak: Cut from the abdominal region, it is often tough, and has a distinctive texture. Usually sliced across the grain for serving.

Short plate
Cut from the diaphragm portion of the underside. This tough cut requires long cooking; it is not called for in this volume.

Brisket
Cut from the breast and foreleg. This tough cut requires long cooking to become tender; it is not called for in this volume.

VEAL

Shoulder
Cut from the shoulder of the carcass, it includes neck, blade, arm, and some ribs. Generally tough meat, suitable for stews, but also some roasts and steaks.

Shoulder steak: Cut from the arm or shoulder blade, and slightly less tender than other veal steaks.

Rib
Cut from the front portion of the carcass, directly behind the shoulder, lying along the backbone. It can be cut into roasts, or into chops to braise or pan fry.

Rib chops: Cut from ribs. Chops cut nearer the shoulder have more bone and fat than those nearer the loin.

Loin
Cut from the mid-portion of the carcass, just in front of the hips, lying along the backbone. It includes roasts, chops, and the sirloin.

Loin chops: Cut from the short loin, they contain tenderloin and are the tenderest cut of veal.

Leg
Cut from the rear leg and rump, it includes round, rump, hindshank, and sirloin tip. Very lean meat, it is used for roasts, steaks, and boneless cutlets.

Cutlets: Thin, boneless slices cut from the leg, about ¼ to ½ inch thick. Very lean, mild-tasting meat. Sometimes known as BONELESS VEAL LEG TOP or BOTTOM STEAK.

Boneless top or bottom round: A cone-shaped roast cut from the leg. Sometimes known as VEAL LEG ROUND ROAST.

Sirloin tip: Cut from tip, a muscle lying between sirloin and round. Sometimes sold as VEAL LEG ROUND ROAST.

Flank
Cut from the belly portion of the underside, it is relatively tough; it is not called for in this volume.

Breast
Cut from the breast and belly portions of the underside, it is relatively fatty and tough, and is roasted and stuffed; it is not called for in this volume.

Foreshank
Cut from the foreleg, it is tough and needs long braising to become tender; it is not called for in this volume.

VARIETY MEATS
These include both beef and calf tongue, brains, kidneys, and sweetbreads. They are all delicate and easily perishable.

Sweetbreads: The twin-lobed thymus gland. They often need to be soaked and blanched.

the lower leg and shoulder require moist-heat cooking to make the meat more tender. Some of the delicate rib, loin, and rump cuts can be cooked by dry heat if the heat is kept low; otherwise the meat toughens and dries out.

IDENTIFYING CUTS OF BEEF AND VEAL

Carcasses of beef are split in two sides, including a forequarter and a hindquarter, from which come the primal cuts, that is, the seven wholesale cuts: chuck (shoulder), rib, loin, round, flank, short plate, and brisket. Each primal cut is further subdivided into the smaller retail cuts, such as roasts and steaks. Veal cuts closely resemble those of beef, but are on a smaller scale. To avoid confusion, you should learn to recognize retail cuts by sight rather than by name. However, the Meat Board has developed a standardized nomenclature system that many retail markets use, and that is followed in this volume.

STORING BEEF AND VEAL

All fresh meat requires cold-temperature storage to prevent flavor deterioration and spoilage. If you plan to cook cuts of beef and veal within a few days of purchase, you should store them preferably in the original store wrapper, or rewrap them and put them in the coldest section of your refrigerator. Do not rinse the meat before storing it. You can safely refrigerate large pieces of beef or veal for three to four days, and smaller pieces for two to three days. Because they spoil very quickly, do not refrigerate ground meats and variety meats for more than one to two days.

To freeze meat properly, the freezer should be set at −10 degrees F, and the temperature raised to zero degrees F after the meat is frozen. The freezing compartment of a one-door refrigerator is not cold enough to freeze meat and should only be used to store meat in an emergency for up to one week, or for pre-frozen meat. To freeze meat, enfold it in plastic freezer wrap or specially coated freezer paper. The wrapping must be airtight to seal in moisture and keep out air. This prevents freezer burn, which creates a brown, dried out surface that must be cut off when the meat thaws. Do not wrap meat in aluminum foil because it can tear easily, allowing air to reach the meat. Label and date each package with a waterproof marker. Rotate meats so that older cuts do not get overlooked. The maximum freezing time for beef is 12 months, but for best flavor, you should use it in six to nine months. Freeze veal for no more than four to six months. You can freeze ground beef and variety meats for up to three months.

To thaw frozen meats, loosen the wrapping, but do not uncover completely, and set in your refrigerator for 24 to 72 hours in a tray or dish. If you intend to marinate frozen meat, unwrap it and let it thaw in the marinade. Cook meat as soon as possible after it thaws.

COOKING TECHNIQUES

Sautéing

Sautéing is a form of quick frying, with no cover on the pan. In French, *sauter* means "to jump," which is what vegetables or small pieces of food do when you shake the sauté pan. The purpose is to lightly brown the food and seal in the juices, sometimes before further cooking. This technique has three critical elements: the right pan, the proper temperature, and dry food.

The sauté pan: A proper sauté pan is 10 to 12 inches in diameter and has 2- to 3-inch straight sides that allow you to turn food pieces and still keep the fat from spattering. It has a heavy bottom that slides easily over a burner.

The best material (and the most expensive) for a sauté pan is tin-lined copper because it is a superior heat conductor. Heavy-gauge aluminum works well but will discolor acidic food like tomatoes. Therefore, you should not use aluminum if the food is to be cooked for more than twenty minutes after the initial browning. Another option is to select a heavy-duty sauté pan made of strong, heat-conductive aluminum alloys. This type of professional cookware is smooth and stick-resistant.

Select a sauté pan large enough to hold the pieces of food without crowding. The heat of the fat and the air spaces around and between the pieces facilitate browning. Crowding results in steaming—a technique that lets the juices out rather than sealing them in. If your sauté pan is not large enough to prevent crowding, separate the food into two batches, or use two pans at once.

Be sure you buy a sauté pan with a tight-fitting cover. Many recipes call for sautéing first, then lowering the heat and cooking the food, covered, for an additional 10 to 20 minutes. Make certain the handle is long and is comfortable to hold.

Never immerse the hot pan in cold water because this will warp the metal. Allow the pan to cool slightly, then add water and let it sit until you are ready to wash it. Use a wooden spatula or tongs to keep food pieces moving in the pan as you shake it over the burner. If the food sticks, as it occasionally will, a metal spatula will loosen it best. Turn the pieces so that all surfaces come into contact with the hot fat and none of them sticks. Do not use a fork when sautéing meat; piercing the meat will toughen it.

The fat: A combination of half butter and half vegetable oil or peanut oil is perfect for most sautéing: it heats to high temperatures without burning and allows you to have a rich butter flavor at the same time. Always use unsalted butter for cooking, since it tastes better and does not add unwanted salt to your recipe.

Butter alone makes a wonderful-tasting sauté, but butter, whether salted or unsalted, burns at a high temperature. If you prefer an all-butter flavor, clarify the butter before you begin. This mean removing the milky residue, which is the part that scorches. To clarify butter, heat it in a small saucepan over medium heat and, using a cooking spoon, skim off the foam as it rises to the top and discard it. Keep skimming until no more foam appears. Pour off the remaining oil, making sure to leave the milky residue at the bottom of the pan. The oil is clarified butter; use this for sautés. Ideally, you should clarify butter a batch at a time. But it is a simple matter to make a large quantity of it and store it in your refrigerator; it will keep for two to three weeks. Some sautéing recipes in this book call for olive oil, which imparts a delicious and distinctive flavor of its own and is less sensitive than butter to high heat. Nevertheless, even the finest olive oil has some residue of fruit pulp, which will scorch over high heat. Watch carefully when you sauté in olive oil; discard any scorched oil and start with fresh if necessary.

To sauté properly, heat the sauté fat until it is hot but not smoking. When you see small bubbles on top of the fat, it is almost hot enough to smoke. In that case, lower the heat. When using butter and oil together, add the butter to the hot oil. After the foam from the melting butter subsides, you are ready to sauté. If the temperature is just right, the food will sizzle when you put it in.

Steaming

A fast and nutritious way to cook vegetables, steaming is also an excellent method for cooking meat or fish. Bring water, or a combination of stock and wine, to a boil in a steamer. Place the food in the steaming-basket or rack over the liquid, and cover the pan—periodically checking the water level. Keeping the food above the liquid preserves vitamins and minerals.

Stir Frying

This is the basic cooking method for Chinese cuisine. This fast-cook method requires very little oil, and the foods—which you stir continuously—fry quickly over a very high heat. This is ideal for cooking bite-size shredded or thinly sliced portions of vegetables, fish, meat, or poultry alone or in combination. Norman Weinstein (page 52) uses this cooking method for his Beef with Shredded Vegetables.

A NOTE ABOUT GROUND BEEF

Strictly speaking, ground beef is not a retail cut, but most butchers and supermarkets package ground beef according to the source of meat: sirloin, round, and chuck. It is actually called ground beef if it is composed of a mixture of trimmings from all primal cuts. However, in cooking with ground meats, the amount of fat rather than the origin of the beef determines the taste and tenderness. Therefore, some markets now label their ground meat according to its fat content rather than its origin. Because of its higher fat content many people prefer ground chuck, although ground beef is highest in fat; those counting calories should select ground round, the leanest of all ground meats.

Some butchers grind trimmings of varying degrees of freshness with fresh meat, which explains why ground beef sometimes has patches of gray and brown. For optimum freshness, select a piece of meat and have the butcher grind it for you. Never sample raw ground beef while you are seasoning it for cooking. Pregnant women should never eat raw meat.

Deglazing

To deglaze a pan in which meat has been cooked means simply to remove the food and to pour off any fat in excess of one or two tablespoons and then, with the pan over medium heat on top of the range, to pour liquid into it—stock, water, or wine—and reduce the liquid. As this liquid reduces, you scrape the sides and bottom of the pan with a long-handled spoon (wooden if possible) to pick up any tiny bits of brown meat, congealed juices, herbs, and any other good things clinging to the pan.

Poaching

You poach meat, fish, or chicken, even fruit, exactly as you would an egg, in very hot liquid in a shallow pan on top of the stove. You can use water, or better still, beef, chicken, or fish stock, or a combination of stock and white wine, or even cream. Bring the liquid to the simmering point and add the food. Be prepared to lower the heat if the liquid begins to boil. Lengthy boiling toughens meat and dries it out. See Mary Beth Clark's Medallions of Rare Tenderloin à la Ficelle (pages 76–77).

Searing

Searing is somewhat like sautéing, but you need slightly hotter fat; when you sear, you brown the meat without shaking or stirring the pan. Heat the oil until it is very hot (at least 350 degrees), then brown the meat over high heat for a minute or two on each side. A metal spatula is essential, for the meat will tend to stick. Never pierce the meat; otherwise juices will be released and the meat will become dry and tough. Wait until it is very brown before you turn it.

Deep-Fat Frying

The best way to fry is to heat the fat slowly to between 360 and 375 degrees in a deep cast-iron skillet or other heavy, high-sided pan. Use a deep-fat thermometer or test the temperature by frying a small cube of bread—it should brown in less than a minute when the fat is hot enough. The temperature is important; underheating causes the food to absorb oil, and overheating scorches it.

The fat should be vegetable or peanut oil; never use butter alone or a mostly butter mixture. Whatever fat you use, slide the pieces of food gently into the pan.

Broiling and Grilling

These are two relatively fast ways to cook meat, poultry, and fish, giving the food a crisp exterior while leaving the inside juicy. For uniform cooking, flatten the pieces of food to an even thickness. Whether broiling or grilling, brush meat with melted fat, a sauce, or a marinade before you cook. This adds flavor and keeps the food moist.

In broiling, the meat cooks directly under the heat source. To ensure proper cooking, move the broiling rack five or six inches from the heat source.

In grilling, the food cooks either directly over a bed of charcoal or on a well-seasoned cast-iron or stoneware griddle placed directly over a burner. The griddle is heated until splashed-on drops of cold water jump. Jim Fobel cooks onion slices using this method (page 37).

Making Stocks

Although canned chicken broth or stock is all right for emergencies, homemade chicken stock has a rich flavor that is hard to match. Moreover, the commercial broths—particularly the canned ones—are likely to be oversalted.

To make your own stock, save chicken parts as they accumulate and put them in a bag in the freezer; then have a rainy-day stock-making session, using the recipe below. The skin from a yellow onion will add color; the optional veal bone will add extra flavor and richness to the stock.

Chicken Stock

3 pounds bony chicken parts, such as wings, back, and neck
1 veal knuckle (optional)
3 quarts cold water
1 yellow unpeeled onion, stuck with 2 cloves
2 stalks celery with leaves, cut in two
12 crushed peppercorns
2 carrots, scraped and cut into 2-inch lengths
4 sprigs parsley
1 bay leaf
1 tablespoon fresh thyme, or 1 teaspoon dried
Salt (optional)

1. Wash chicken parts and veal knuckle (if you are using it) and drain. Place in large soup kettle or stockpot (any big pot) with the remaining ingredients—except salt. Cover pot and bring to a boil over medium heat.
2. Lower heat and simmer stock, partly covered, 2 to 3 hours. Skim foam and scum from top of stock several times. Add salt to taste after stock has cooked 1 hour.
3. Strain stock through fine sieve placed over large bowl. Discard chicken pieces, vegetables, and seasonings. Let stock cool uncovered (this will speed cooling process). When completely cool, refrigerate. Fat will rise and congeal conveniently at top. You may skim it off and discard it or leave it as protective covering for stock.

Beef stock, although time-consuming to make, requires very little attention while cooking. Use marrow bones and an inexpensive cut of beef, such as shin, in roughly equal amounts. If you use beef knuckle, have the butcher saw it into quarters. During the first few minutes of cooking, the beef and bones will produce a scum that must be carefully removed from the surface, but for the bulk of the cooking time, the stock will require only occasional skimming. The cooking time given is approximate. Long, slow simmering is necessary to extract all the flavor from the ingredients, but a half hour more or less will not matter significantly. When the stock is cooked, leave it uncovered at room temperature until it is completely cool: Stock will turn sour if it is covered while still warm. Stock may be refrigerated for several days or frozen for up to three months.

Beef Stock

1 leek (optional)
2 medium-size carrots
3 to 4 celery stalks with leaves
6 to 8 sprigs fresh parsley
1½ teaspoons chopped fresh thyme or ½ to ¾ teaspoon dried
Large onion
3 cloves garlic (optional)
2 pounds shin of beef with bone
2 pounds marrow bones, or 1 pound marrow bones and 1 beef knuckle
1 bay leaf
6 whole cloves (optional)
8 peppercorns
1½ teaspoons salt

1. Trim and clean leek; peel carrots, wash celery and parsley; chop fresh thyme, if using. Do not peel onion and garlic.
2. Place beef and bones in kettle and add approximately 4 quarts of cold water, to cover beef and bones by about 2 inches. Over moderate heat, bring to a simmer, skimming off scum as it rises.
3. When scum has almost stopped surfacing, add vegetables, herbs, and seasonings and return to a simmer. Partially cover pot and, over low heat, cook stock at a gentle simmer, skimming as necessary, approximately 4 to 5 hours.
4. Taste stock. Cook down further if flavor needs to be intensified, or add water if it has reduced too much and the flavor is too strong.
5. Strain stock through fine sieve into large bowl or jar. Discard bones, meat, vegetables, and seasonings. Allow stock to cool completely, uncovered.
6. Refrigerate stock until a layer of fat has solidified on surface. Remove it with a spoon and discard it. Return defatted stock to refrigerator, or freeze, for future use.

Roasting and Baking

Originally, *roasting* was the term for cooking meat on a revolving spit over an open fire, but now it means cooking meat or poultry in an oven by a dry-heat process. Roasting is especially suitable for thick cuts of meat and whole poultry. You should baste meats several times with drippings or a flavorful basting sauce as with Victoria Fahey's Oven-Barbecued Beef Back Ribs (page 62).

Baking also means cooking food in the oven, but it is a much more versatile technique. You use it for preparing breads and raw vegetables or for cooking a combination of foods as with Stevie Bass's Veal in Gougère (page 23), or for salt baking, that is, burying meat, fish or poultry in coarse salt.

Braising

This method cooks food by moist heat, but you generally brown the food well before combining it with the cooking liquid. Then you simmer the food and the liquid slowly over low heat. Braising is a fine way to tenderize tough cuts of meat, and it also produces delicious vegetable dishes. See Jack Ubaldi's Braised Celery (page 73).

Pan Frying

The food cooks, uncovered, in a small amount of fat, which has been preheated in a heavy skillet. Pan frying is a quick cooking method—it is suitable for thin-cut chops, steaks, and other foods. See Stevie Bass's Steak with Pesto and Sour Cream (page 27) as an example.

Pantry (for this volume)

A well-stocked, properly organized pantry is essential for preparing great meals in the shortest time possible. Whether your pantry consists of a small refrigerator and two or three shelves over the sink, or a large freezer, refrigerator, and entire room just off the kitchen, you must protect staples from heat and light.

In maintaining your pantry, follow these rules:

1. Store staples by kind and date. Canned goods, canisters, and spices need a separate shelf, or a separate spot on a shelf. Date all staples—shelved, refrigerated, or frozen—by writing the date directly on the package or on a bit of masking tape. Then put the oldest ones in front to be sure you use them first.

2. Store flour, sugar, and other dry ingredients in canisters or jars with tight lids. Glass and clear plastic allow you to see at a glance how much remains.

3. Keep a running grocery list so that you can note when a staple is half gone, and be sure to stock up.

ON THE SHELF:

Anchovies

Anchovy fillets, both flat and rolled, come oil-packed in tins. If you buy salt-packed anchovies, sold in bulk or large tins, they must be cleaned under cold running water, skinned, and boned. To bone, part the fish with your fingers and slip out the backbone.

Baking powder

Baking soda

Bouquet garni

This is an herb bouquet most often composed of parsley, thyme, and bay leaf. If you are using fresh herbs, tie them together with string; if dried, tie them in a square of washed cheesecloth. A *bouquet garni* is always removed from the dish before serving.

Capers

Capers are usually packed in vinegar and less frequently in salt. If you use the latter, you should rinse them under cold water before using them.

Cornstarch

Less likely to lump than flour, cornstarch is an excellent thickener for sauces and may be substituted in the following proportions: 1 tablespoon cornstarch to 2 of flour.

Crème fraîche

Dried fruits

raisins, dark and golden

Flour

all-purpose, bleached or
    unbleached

cornmeal

May be yellow or white and of various degrees of coarseness. The stone-ground variety, milled to retain the germ of the corn, generally has a superior flavor.

Garlic

Store in a cool, dry, well-ventilated place. Garlic powder and garlic salt are not adequate substitutes for fresh garlic.

Herbs and spices

The flavor of fresh herbs is much better than that of dried. Fresh herbs should be refrigerated and used as soon as possible. The following herbs are perfectly acceptable dried, but buy in small amounts, store airtight in dry area away from heat and light, and use as quickly as possible. In measuring herbs, remember that one part dried will equal three parts fresh. *Note:* Dried chives and parsley should not be on your shelf, since they have little or no flavor; frozen chives are acceptable. Buy whole spices rather than ground, as they keep their flavor much longer. Grind spices at home and store as directed for herbs.

allspice
basil
bay leaves
caraway seeds
Cayenne pepper
chervil
chili powder

cinnamon, sticks and
    ground
cloves, whole and ground
coriander
cumin
curry powder, preferably
    imported
dill
fennel seed
ginger
marjoram
mint
mustard (powdered)
nutmeg, whole and ground
oregano
paprika
pepper

black peppercorns

These are unripe peppercorns dried in their husks. Grind with a pepper mill for each use.

white peppercorns

These are the same as the black variety, but are picked ripe and husked. Use them in pale sauces when black pepper specks would spoil the appearance.

poppy seed
red pepper flakes (also
    called crushed red
    pepper)
rosemary
saffron

Made from the dried stigmas of a species of crocus, this spice—the most costly of all seasonings—adds both color and flavor.

sage
salt

Use coarse salt—commonly available as Kosher or sea—for its superior flavor, texture, and purity. Kosher salt and sea salt are less salty than table salt. Substitute in the following proportions: three quarters teaspoon table salt equals one teaspoon Kosher or sea salt.

savory
sesame seeds
tarragon
thyme

***Hoisin* sauce**

An important ingredient in Chinese cooking, it is a sweet soybean-based sauce with vinegar and spices.

Honey

Hot pepper sauce

Maifun (rice sticks)

Maple syrup

Nuts, whole or chopped

almonds
pecans
walnuts

Oils

corn, safflower, or
    vegetable

Because these neutral-tasting oils have high smoking points, they are good for high-heat sautéing.

olive oil

Sample French, Greek, Spanish, and Italian oils. Olive oil ranges in color from pale yellow to dark green and in taste from mild and delicate to rich and fruity. Different olive oils can be used for different purposes: lighter ones for cooking, stronger ones for salads. The finest quality olive oil is labeled extra virgin or virgin.

Olives, green and black

Onions

Store all dry-skinned onions in a cool, dry, well-ventilated place.

Bermuda onions
Large and mild, with a flattish shape, they are best baked whole or eaten raw, although they can be used in cooking. They are generally yellow but also may be red or white.

red or Italian onions
Zesty tasting and generally eaten raw. The perfect salad onion.

shallots
The most subtle member of the onion family, the shallot has a delicate garlic flavor.

Spanish onions
Very large with a sweet flavor, they are best for stuffing and baking and are also eaten raw. Perfect for sandwiches.

Yellow onions
All-purpose cooking onions, strong in taste.

White onions
Also called "silverskins," these small onions are almost always cooked and served whole.

Pasta and noodles

The general rule—though by no means hard and fast—is to match heavier pastas to more substantial sauces and lighter pastas to lighter sauces.

Potatoes

"New" potatoes are not a particular kind of potato, but any potato that has not been stored.

Rice

Arborio rice
A plump, short-grain rice that turns creamy-firm when cooked. It is ideal for risotto, paella, and puddings. Available in Italian groceries, specialty food stores, and some supermarkets.

long-grain white rice
Slender grains, much longer than they are wide, that become light and fluffy when cooked and are best for general use.

Soy sauce

Stock, chicken and beef

For maximum flavor and quality, your own stock is best (see recipe page 13), but canned stock, or broth, is adequate for most recipes and convenient to have on hand.

Sugar

brown sugar
confectioners' sugar
granulated sugar

Tomatoes

Italian plum tomatoes
Canned plum tomatoes (preferably imported) are an acceptable substitute for fresh when making tomato sauces.

tomato paste
Also for sauces. Spoon single tablespoons of unused canned paste onto wax paper and freeze them. Lift frozen paste off and store in plastic container. Sometimes available in tubes, which can be stored in the refrigerator after a small amount is used.

tomato sauce

Vanilla extract

Use pure, not imitation, extract.

Vinegars

apple cider vinegar (also called cider vinegar)
Use for a mild, fruity flavor.

balsamic vinegar
Aged vinegar with a complex sweet and sour taste.

red and white wine vinegars

sherry wine vinegar
Somewhat less sharp than most wine vinegars, it has a deeper, fuller flavor. Buy in specialty stores.

tarragon vinegar
A white wine vinegar flavored with fresh tarragon, it is especially good in salads.

Wines and brandies

Brandy or Cognac
Madeira
Marsala
red wine, dry
sherry, sweet and dry
white wine, dry

Worcestershire sauce

Bread crumbs

You need never buy bread crumbs. To make fresh crumbs, use fresh or day-old bread and process in food processor or blender. For dried, toast bread 30 minutes in preheated 250-degree oven, turning occasionally to prevent slices from browning. Proceed as for fresh. Store bread crumbs in an airtight container: fresh crumbs in the refrigerator, and dried crumbs in a cool, dry place. Either type may also be frozen for several weeks if tightly wrapped in a plastic bag.

Butter

Many cooks prefer unsalted butter because of its finer flavor and because it does not burn as easily as salted.

Cheese

cream cheese

mozzarella
A mild cheese, most commonly made from cow's milk. Fresh mozzarella is far superior to packaged and can generally be found in Italian grocery stores.

Parmesan cheese
Avoid the preground packaged variety; it is very expensive and almost flavorless. Buy Parmesan by the quarter- or half-pound wedge and grate as needed: 4 ounces produces approximately one cup of grated cheese. Romano, far less costly, can be substituted if necessary, but its flavor is considerably sharper—or try mixing the two.

Provolone
Use imported if possible.

ricotta cheese
This delicate, soft cheese, which resembles good-quality small-curd cottage cheese, is a by-product of whey. It is available fresh or dry (*ricotta salata*).

Cream

half-and-half
heavy cream
sour cream

Eggs

Will keep 4 to 5 weeks in refrigerator. For best results, bring to room temperature before using.

Ginger, fresh

Found in the produce section. Ginger will stay fresh in the refrigerator for approximately 1 week, wrapped in plastic. To preserve it longer, place the whole ginger root in a small sherry-filled jar; it will last almost indefinitely, although not without changes in the ginger. Or, if you prefer, store it in the freezer, where it will last about 3 months. Newly purchased ginger need not be peeled.

Lemons

In addition to its many uses in cooking, a slice of lemon rubbed over cut apples and pears will keep them from discoloring. Do not substitute bottled juice or lemon extract.

Mayonnaise

Milk

Mustards

Dry mustard and regular hot dog mustard have their uses and their devotees, but the recipes in this book call for Dijon or coarse-ground mustard.

Parsley

The two most commonly available kinds of parsley are flat-leaved and curly; they can be used interchangeably when necessary. Flat-leaved parsley has a more distinctive flavor and is generally preferred in cooking. Curly parsley wilts less easily and is excellent for garnishing. Store parsley in a glass of water and cover loosely with a plastic bag. It will keep for a week in the refrigerator. Or wash and dry it, and refrigerate in a small plastic bag with a dry paper towel inside to absorb any moisture.

Scallions

Scallions have a mild onion flavor. Store wrapped in plastic.

Equipment

Proper cooking equipment makes the work light and is a good cook's most prized possession. You can cook expertly without a store-bought steamer or even a food processor, but basic pans, knives, and a few other items are indispensable. Below are the things you need—and some attractive options—for preparing the menus in this volume.

Pots and pans
Large kettle or stockpot
3 skillets (large, medium, small), with covers
Sauté pans, 10 to 12 inches in diameter, with covers and oven-proof handles
14-inch wok
3 saucepans with covers (1-, 2-, and 4-quart capacities)
Choose enameled cast-iron, plain cast-iron, aluminum-clad stainless steel, and heavy aluminum (but you need at least one saucepan that is not aluminum). Best—but very expensive—is tin-lined copper.
Roasting pan with rack
Broiler pan
2 shallow baking pans (8 x 8 x 2-inch, and 13 x 9 x 2-inch)
2 cookie sheets (11 x 17-inch and 15½ x 12-inch)
Four 7½ x 4½ x 1½-inch oval ceramic gratin dishes
2- or 3-quart casserole with cover
9-inch or 10-inch pie plate
2 cake pans (9-inch diameter)

Knives
A carbon-steel knife takes a sharp edge but tends to rust. You must wash and dry it after each use; otherwise it can blacken foods and counter tops. Good-quality stainless steel knives, frequently honed, are less trouble and will serve just as well in the home kitchen. Never put a fine knife in the dishwasher. Rinse it, dry it, and put it away—but not loose in a drawer.
Small paring knife
10-inch chef's knife
Thin-bladed slicing knife
Sharpening steel

Other cooking tools
2 sets of mixing bowls in graduated sizes
Flour sifter
Colander, with a round base (stainless steel, aluminum, or enamel)
Strainers (preferably 2, in fine and coarse mesh)
Sieve, coarse mesh
2 sets of measuring cups and spoons in graduated sizes
One for dry ingredients, another for shortenings and liquids.
Long-handled cooking spoon
Long-handled slotted spoon
2 long-handled wooden spoons
Long-handled, 2-pronged fork
Wooden spatula (for stirring hot ingredients)
Metal spatula, or turner (for lifting hot foods from pans)
Chinese metal wok spatulas
Metal flexible-blade spatula
Rubber or vinyl spatula (for folding in ingredients)
Grater (metal, with several sizes of holes)
A rotary grater is handy for hard cheese.
2 wire whisks
Pair of metal tongs
Wooden chopping board
Food mill, ricer, or potato masher
Vegetable steamer
Vegetable peeler
Mortar and pestle
Soup ladle
Four 8- to 10-inch metal or bamboo skewers
Nutcracker
Kitchen scissors
Kitchen timer
Kitchen string
Toothpicks
Aluminum foil
Cheesecloth
Paper towels
Plastic wrap
Wax paper

Electric appliances
Blender or food processor
A blender will do most of the work required in this volume, but a food processor will do it more quickly and in larger volume. A food processor should be considered a necessity, not a luxury, for anyone who enjoys cooking.
Electric mixer

Optional
Griddle
Double boiler
Gratin dish
Custard cups
Copper bowl
Salad spinner
Bread knife (serrated edge)
Carving knife
Citrus juicer
Inexpensive glass kind from the dime store will do.
Melon baller
Pastry brush for basting
A small, new paintbrush that is not nylon serves well.
Pastry blender
Rolling pin
Flame tamer or asbestos mat
Meat grinder
Garlic press
Zester
Roll of masking tape or white paper tape for labeling and dating

STOCKPOT

SHARPENING STEEL

MEAT THERMOMETER

BREAD KNIFE

CHEF'S KNIFE

PARING KNIFE

SLOTTED SPATULA

STEAMER

GRATER

WHISK

RUBBER SPATULA

CITRUS JUICER

DOUBLE BOILER

SAUCEPANS

METAL TONGS

SLOTTED SPOON

SAUTÉ PAN

SIEVE

17

Stevie Bass

When cooking for her own pleasure, food consultant Stevie Bass experiments with unusual ingredients and unexpected flavor combinations. Her goal is to create harmonious meals that balance color, texture, and flavor. Although the finished product may look complicated, Stevie Bass's recipes require minimal fuss. In Menu 1, an Oriental meal, she features two popular Vietnamese dishes. Asparagus (introduced to Vietnam by the French, and known there as "Western bamboo") is paired with crab meat to create a light, refreshing soup. The main course—beef balls and noodles seasoned with soy sauce and ginger and then wrapped in lettuce packages—is traditionally served as an appetizer in Vietnam. To accompany them, Stevie Bass offers a choice of sweet-spicy dipping sauces.

Both Menu 2 and Menu 3 are easy meals but elegant enough for guests. Menu 2 features a delicately seasoned veal and vegetable stew in a cream-puff pastry crust. In Menu 3, Stevie Bass combines steak and veal sweetbread kabobs with stir-fried fresh vegetables and a green salad dressed with a mustard-flavored glaze. Menu 4 features Stevie Bass's version of an Italian classic—pesto. Pesto is most often used for pasta; in this dish, it accompanies pan-fried sirloin steaks.

Serve this Oriental meal buffet fashion, and let your guests help themselves by ladling crab meat and asparagus soup into bowls, then removing the beef balls from the skewers and wrapping them in lettuce leaves, Vietnamese style. Maifun noodles, mint leaves, scallions, and a dipping sauce for the lettuce packages are also on the buffet table. Garnish the snow pea, mushroom, and cherry tomato salad with toasted sesame seeds.

Crab and Asparagus Soup
Vietnamese Lettuce-Wrap Beef
Snow Peas and Mushrooms with Tangy Dressing

Wrapping food in leaves is an ancient custom, particularly in Southeast Asia. For this version, each person takes the beef balls off the skewer, then puts one or two of the balls on a lettuce leaf, adds fresh mint leaves, scallions, and noodles to taste, and then folds the package up. It is then dipped in a sauce.

Mint is an integral part of the flavor balance here, but you may substitute fresh celery leaves or parsley. Also known as rice noodles or rice sticks, *maifun* are thin ivory-colored noodles made from rice flour. Chinese groceries and some supermarkets sell them. You can substitute Japanese ramen noodles, which are available in the soup section of most supermarkets.

The sauce shown here is made from apricot nectar combined with Chinese *hoisin* sauce. You will find *hoisin* in many supermarkets and in Chinese groceries.

WHAT TO DRINK

With the Oriental spices and the strong fruit flavor of the sauces, try a soft slightly sweet white wine such as a light German Riesling or a California Chenin Blanc.

SHOPPING LIST AND STAPLES

1¼ to 1½ pounds lean ground beef
¼ pound fresh crab meat, or 6-ounce can
1 pound asparagus
½ pound fresh snow peas, or two 6-ounce packages frozen
¼ pound mushrooms
1 pint cherry tomatoes
1 head iceberg lettuce (about 1 pound)
1 bunch scallions
Small bunch fresh coriander
1 bunch fresh mint
1¼-inch piece fresh ginger
3 large cloves garlic, plus 1 large clove (optional)
Small fresh peach (optional)
1 egg
3½ cups chicken stock, preferably homemade (see page 13), or canned
5½-ounce can apricot nectar
⅓ cup plus 2 tablespoons vegetable oil
½ cup *hoisin* sauce
4½ tablespoons soy sauce, plus 3 tablespoons (optional)
2 tablespoons white wine vinegar
7 ounces rice stick (*maifun*) or *ramen* noodles

2 tablespoons sugar, plus 1 tablespoon (optional)
3 tablespoons cornstarch
1 tablespoon sesame seeds
Freshly ground pepper

UTENSILS

Blender
Small heavy-gauge skillet
Large saucepan
Medium-size saucepan
Broiler pan
Large mixing bowl
Large salad bowl
2 small bowls
Colander
Salad spinner (optional)
Measuring cups and spoons
Chef's knife
Paring knife
Wooden spoon
Metal spatula
Grater
Whisk
Four 10-inch metal or bamboo skewers

START-TO-FINISH STEPS

At least 30 minutes ahead: If using bamboo skewers for lettuce wrap recipe, soak them in water to reduce charring.

1. Peel and mince garlic for soup and lettuce wrap recipes. Peel and grate ginger for lettuce wrap and snow peas recipes. Follow snow peas recipe steps 1 through 5.
2. Follow lettuce wrap recipe steps 1 through 6.
3. Chop coriander and follow crab and asparagus soup recipe steps 1 through 6. Serve soup.
4. Follow lettuce wrap recipe steps 7 and 8 and serve with snow peas.

RECIPES

Crab and Asparagus Soup

1 pound asparagus
Large clove garlic
2 scallions
2 tablespoons vegetable oil

¼ pound fresh crab meat, picked over, or 6-ounce can,
  well-drained
3½ cups chicken stock
3 tablespoons cornstarch
1 egg
Freshly ground pepper
2 tablespoons chopped fresh coriander

1. Wash asparagus. Trim and peel, if desired. In large saucepan, combine asparagus with ½ inch water, cover pan, and bring to a boil over high heat. Cook just until crisp-tender, 4 to 12 minutes; cooking time will vary with size. Drain, cut into 2-inch lengths, and set aside.
2. Peel and mince garlic. Wash, trim, and chop enough scallions to measure ¼ cup.
3. In saucepan used for asparagus, heat oil over medium-high heat. Add garlic and half the scallions and sauté until tender, about 2 minutes. Turn heat to high, add crab meat, and, stirring with wooden spoon, sauté about 3 minutes. Pour in chicken stock and bring to a boil.
4. In small bowl, blend cornstarch with 2 tablespoons cold water. Add mixture to boiling soup, stirring constantly, until soup thickens, 1 to 2 minutes. Rinse out bowl.
5. In rinsed bowl, whisk egg briefly and stir into boiling soup. Cook, stirring, about 1 minute. Add asparagus and cook just until heated through. Season to taste with pepper.
6. Transfer soup to serving bowl and sprinkle with coriander and remaining scallions.

Vietnamese Lettuce-Wrap Beef

The beef balls and wrap:
1 head iceberg lettuce (about 1 pound)
1 bunch mint
3 scallions
2 large cloves garlic, peeled and minced
1¼ to 1½ pounds lean ground beef
3 tablespoons soy sauce
¾ teaspoon peeled and grated fresh ginger

1 cup rice stick *(maifun)* or *ramen* noodles (without soup
  seasoning)

The apricot-hoisin sauce:
½ cup apricot nectar
½ cup *hoisin* sauce

The peach-ginger sauce (optional):
Small fresh peach
3 tablespoons soy sauce
¾-inch piece fresh ginger
Large clove garlic, peeled
1 tablespoon sugar

1. Core lettuce and separate into leaves. Wash lettuce leaves and mint, and dry in salad spinner or pat dry with paper towels. Strip enough leaves from mint stems to measure ¾ cup. Wash and trim scallions. Cut crosswise into ⅛-inch rounds. Put lettuce leaves, mint, and scallions in separate serving bowls and set aside.

2. In large bowl, combine beef, garlic, soy sauce, and ginger. Shape into 24 balls of uniform size, 1 to 1½ inches in diameter. String on metal or bamboo skewers.
3. In medium-size saucepan used for snow peas, bring 1 quart water to a boil. Add noodles. Return to a boil and cook 3 minutes. Drain noodles in colander and rinse with cold water to remove starchiness. Turn into serving bowl.
4. Preheat broiler.
5. For apricot-*hoisin* sauce, combine apricot nectar with *hoisin* sauce in small serving bowl and stir until blended.
6. For peach-ginger sauce, if using, wash and pit peach; do not peel. In blender, combine peach, soy sauce, ginger, garlic, and sugar. Process until smooth. Pour into small serving bowl.
7. Place skewers on broiler pan. Broil approximately 3 inches from heating element about 5 minutes, turning skewers once or twice. Transfer to serving platter.
8. Bring the beef balls, lettuce, scallions, mint, noodles, apricot-*hoisin* sauce, and peach-ginger sauce, if serving, to the table. Each person serves himself or herself by putting a beef ball on a lettuce leaf, adding the desired ingredients, wrapping the lettuce leaf around them, and then dipping the bundle into either sauce.

Snow Peas and Mushrooms with Tangy Dressing

1 tablespoon sesame seeds
2 tablespoons white wine vinegar
2 tablespoons sugar
1½ teaspoons soy sauce
1 teaspoon fresh ginger, peeled and grated
⅓ cup vegetable oil
2 cups cherry tomatoes
¼ pound mushrooms
½ pound fresh snow peas,
  or two 6-ounce packages frozen

1. In small skillet, toast sesame seeds over medium heat until they turn light brown, about 2 minutes. Stir with metal spatula and shake skillet frequently to keep seeds from burning.
2. For dressing, combine vinegar, sugar, soy sauce, and ginger in blender. With blender running at low speed, add oil in a slow, steady stream and blend until mixture is thick and smooth.
3. Wash cherry tomatoes and halve. Clean mushrooms with damp paper towels and halve.
4. If using fresh snow peas, trim stem ends, pulling along pod to remove "string." In medium-size saucepan, combine snow peas with 1 cup water. Cover pan, bring to a boil, and cook until crisp-tender, about 2 minutes. Drain in colander and refresh under cold running water. If using frozen snow peas, remove from package, place in colander, and hold under hot tap water just long enough to thaw.
5. In salad bowl, combine snow peas, tomatoes, and mushrooms. Sprinkle with toasted sesame seeds, and toss with dressing. Transfer to platter, cover with plastic wrap, and refrigerate until ready to serve.

Sweet Pea Soup
Veal in Gougère
Broccoli Caesar

Sautéed cubes of veal garnished with chopped parsley come to the table in individual pastry-lined baking dishes. They are complemented by a tart broccoli salad. Serve the pea soup for the first course.

The pastry liner for each baking dish is a version of the French *pâte à chou*, or cream-puff pastry: it puffs up as it bakes and holds its shape when it cools. Line the sides of the dishes only, as pastry on the bottom will become soggy. You can bake the pastry several hours in advance, since the veal-and-vegetable filling will reheat it.

WHAT TO DRINK

A light, fruity red wine—a Bardolino or Valpolicella from Italy, or a Beaujolais from France—would be good here.

SHOPPING LIST AND STAPLES

1½ pounds boneless veal top or bottom round, or veal
    sirloin tip (leg round roast), cut into ¾- to 1-inch cubes
2 slices bacon (about 2 ounces)
1 bunch broccoli (about 1 to 1¼ pounds)
½ pound mushrooms
1 lemon
2 large cloves garlic
Small bunch scallions
Small bunch fresh parsley
Small bunch fresh thyme, or ½ teaspoon dried
Small bunch fresh dill, or ¾ teaspoon dried
3 eggs
5 tablespoons unsalted butter
½ pint heavy cream
½ pint sour cream (optional)
¼ pound Parmesan cheese
1-pound polybag frozen whole small onions
17-ounce can sweet peas
1 cup chicken stock, preferably homemade (see page 13),
    or canned
1 tablespoon tomato paste
½ cup olive oil or vegetable oil
3 tablespoons white wine vinegar
½ cup plus 2 tablespoons flour
¼ teaspoon dry mustard
Salt and freshly ground pepper
¾ cup dry red wine

UTENSILS

Blender
Large heavy-gauge skillet
2 medium-size saucepans with covers
Four 7½ x 4½ x 1½-inch oval ceramic gratin dishes

Large bowl
Large salad bowl
Medium-size bowl
Small bowl
Colander
Measuring cups and spoons
Chef's knife
Paring knife
Large metal spoon
Slotted spoon
Wooden spoon
Metal spatula
Flexible-blade spatula
Rubber spatula
Grater

START-TO-FINISH STEPS

1. Follow veal in gougère recipe steps 1 and 2.
2. While gougère is baking, follow broccoli recipe step 1.
3. While broccoli is cooking, follow soup recipe step 1.
4. Follow broccoli recipe step 2.
5. Remove gougère from oven and follow veal recipe steps 3 and 4.
6. Follow soup recipe steps 2 and 3, and serve.
7. Follow veal recipe steps 5 through 7, and serve with broccoli.

RECIPES

Sweet Pea Soup

¼ cup chopped scallions
17-ounce can sweet peas, drained
1 cup chicken stock
⅓ cup parsley sprigs, packed
1½ teaspoons chopped fresh dill or ½ teaspoon dried
½ cup heavy cream
Sour cream for garnish (optional)

1. In blender, combine scallions, peas, stock, parsley, dill, and heavy cream. Turning blender on and off, blend mixture until it is as smooth as possible. When blender clogs, turn it off to push ingredients down before proceeding.
2. Transfer mixture to medium-size saucepan used for broccoli. Heat over medium-low heat until piping hot, stirring often, but do not allow soup to boil.
3. Pour into individual bowls and garnish with a dollop of sour cream, if desired.

Veal in Gougère

5 tablespoons unsalted butter
½ cup plus 2 tablespoons flour
1 tablespoon freshly grated Parmesan cheese
2 eggs
2 slices bacon (about 2 ounces)
1½ pounds boneless veal top or bottom round, or veal sirloin tip, cut into ¾- to 1-inch cubes

1 cup frozen whole small onions, thawed
½ pound mushrooms, cleaned and halved
1 tablespoon tomato paste
Large clove garlic, minced
1½ teaspoons chopped fresh thyme, or ½ teaspoon dried
¾ cup dry red wine
Salt and freshly ground pepper
4 teaspoons chopped fresh parsley

1. Preheat oven to 400 degrees. In medium-size saucepan, bring ½ cup water and 4 tablespoons butter to a boil over medium heat. When butter has melted, remove pan from heat. Add ½ cup flour all at once and Parmesan cheese. Beat vigorously until mixture comes away from sides of pan and forms a ball. Stir in unbeaten eggs, one at a time, beating thoroughly after each addition.
2. Using flexible-blade spatula, spread mixture about ½ inch thick only against sides, not bottom, of baking dishes. Bake until richly golden, about 18 to 20 minutes.
3. Dice bacon and fry in large skillet until crisp. Using slotted spoon, transfer to paper towels.
4. In skillet with bacon fat, melt remaining tablespoon butter over high heat. Add half of the veal cubes and sauté, stirring frequently with metal spatula, until browned, but still pink inside, about 2 minutes. Transfer to large bowl. Repeat with remaining cubes. Cover bowl with foil.
5. For sauce, add onions, mushrooms, tomato paste, garlic, thyme, wine, ½ cup water, salt and pepper to taste to drippings in skillet. Bring to a boil over high heat, then simmer, uncovered, 5 minutes. Add veal and bacon.
6. In small bowl, blend remaining 2 tablespoons flour with ¼ cup water and gradually stir paste into veal mixture. Over medium-high heat, cook mixture, stirring, until thickened, about 2 minutes.
7. Spoon hot veal mixture into pastry-lined dishes, and garnish with parsley.

Broccoli Caesar

1 bunch broccoli (about 1 to 1¼ pounds)
Large clove garlic, peeled and minced
1 tablespoon lemon juice
¼ teaspoon dry mustard
¼ teaspoon salt
Dash of freshly ground pepper
1 egg
3 tablespoons white wine vinegar
½ cup olive oil or vegetable oil

1. Wash broccoli thoroughly and trim. Peel stems, if desired, and cut into spears. In medium-size saucepan, bring 1 inch water to a boil. Add broccoli, cover, and return to a boil. Boil gently 5 to 8 minutes, or until crisp-tender. Drain immediately in colander and refresh under cold running water.
2. In salad bowl, combine garlic, lemon, mustard, salt, pepper, egg, vinegar, and oil. With fork, stir until well blended. Add broccoli and toss gently but thoroughly with dressing. Cover and refrigerate until ready to serve.

Steak and Sweetbread Kabobs
Stir-Fried Vegetables
Green Salad with Mustard Glaze

Arrange the steak and sweetbread kabobs on a large platter, and serve the vegetables and tossed salad on the side.

Fresh veal sweetbreads should be plump and rosy, and encased in a shiny membrane. They are prepared by washing thoroughly, parboiling to firm them, and then removing the membrane. Since they are precooked, the sweetbreads broil as quickly as the steak cubes. Most supermarkets sell sweetbreads.

WHAT TO DRINK

The bright, straightforward flavors of this menu need a simple, robust red wine to accompany them. Try a young California Zinfandel or an Italian or California Barbera.

SHOPPING LIST AND STAPLES

1 pound veal sweetbreads
1 pound boneless beef sirloin (beef loin sirloin steak), cut into 1½-inch cubes
4 bacon slices (about 3 ounces)
1 head Romaine or iceberg lettuce
Large zucchini and large crookneck, or summer, squash (about 1¼ pounds total weight)
1 bunch celery
1 pint cherry tomatoes
2 lemons, plus 1 additional lemon (optional)
4 large cloves garlic

Small bunch fresh parsley (optional)
Small bunch fresh tarragon, or 2 teaspoons dried
1 stick unsalted butter
1 tablespoon Dijon mustard
½ cup plus 2 tablespoons vegetable oil
⅓ cup white wine vinegar
2 teaspoons soy sauce
5 teaspoons sugar
1¼ teaspoons salt
Freshly ground pepper

UTENSILS

Blender
2 medium-size heavy-gauge skillets
Large saucepan
Small saucepan
Broiler pan
Strainer
Salad spinner (optional)
Measuring cups and spoons
Chef's knife
Paring knife
Metal spatula
Basting brush
Four 12-inch metal or bamboo skewers

START-TO-FINISH STEPS

At least 30 minutes ahead: If using bamboo skewers for kabobs, soak them in water to reduce charring.

1. Follow salad recipe steps 1 and 2.
2. Follow kabobs recipe steps 1 and 2 and vegetables recipe step 1.
3. Follow kabobs recipe steps 3 through 5.
4. Follow vegetables recipe step 2.
5. Follow kabobs recipe step 6. Cut several strips of lemon peel for garnish, if using. Immediately after turning skewers, follow vegetables recipe step 3.
6. Follow salad recipe step 3.
7. Follow kabobs recipe step 7 and serve with stir-fried vegetables and salad.

RECIPES

Steak and Sweetbread Kabobs

2 lemons
1 pound veal sweetbreads
1 teaspoon salt
4 bacon slices
1 pound boneless beef sirloin (beef loin sirloin steak), cut into 1½-inch cubes
Freshly ground pepper
2 large cloves garlic, peeled and minced
1 stick unsalted butter
2 tablespoons chopped fresh tarragon, or 2 teaspoons dried, crumbled

1. Squeeze enough lemon to measure 5 tablespoons juice.

Strain to remove pits. Wash sweetbreads in cool water. In large saucepan, combine sweetbreads with 1 quart water, 1 tablespoon lemon juice, and salt. Bring to a boil and simmer, covered, 15 minutes.
2. While sweetbreads are simmering, sauté bacon in skillet just until it begins to brown but is not crisp. Drain on paper towels. Cut into 1-inch lengths.
3. Preheat broiler. Drain sweetbreads in colander and refresh under cold water. Remove white membrane and cut into 1- to 1½-inch chunks.
4. Thread meat onto skewers, alternating beef cubes, bacon, and sweetbreads. Sprinkle with pepper to taste and arrange on broiler pan.
5. In small saucepan, combine butter, tarragon, garlic, and remaining lemon juice. Heat, stirring, just until butter melts. Brush basting sauce lightly over meat.
6. Broil meat approximately 3 inches from heating element 2 to 3 minutes on each side.
7. Transfer kabobs to platter. Pour any remaining tarragon butter into small bowl and serve separately.

Stir-Fried Vegetables

4 celery stalks
Large zucchini and large crookneck, or summer, squash
1 pint cherry tomatoes
2 tablespoons vegetable oil
2 teaspoons soy sauce

1. Wash and dry celery, zucchini, squash, and cherry tomatoes. Cut celery diagonally into ⅛-inch-thick slices. Cut zucchini and squash diagonally into 2-inch pieces, then slice into ⅛-inch julienne. Halve cherry tomatoes.
2. In medium-size skillet, heat oil over medium heat. Add celery, zucchini, and squash, and stir fry until crisp-tender, about 5 minutes.
3. Add tomatoes and soy sauce, and continue cooking just until heated through.

Green Salad with Mustard Glaze

1 head Romaine or iceberg lettuce
2 large cloves garlic, peeled
⅓ cup white wine vinegar
1 tablespoon Dijon mustard
5 teaspoons sugar
¼ teaspoon salt
½ cup vegetable oil

1. Wash lettuce, separate leaves, and dry in salad spinner or pat dry with paper towels. Tear enough leaves into bite-size pieces to measure 6 cups. Place in salad bowl, cover with plastic wrap, and refrigerate until ready to serve.
2. In blender, combine garlic, vinegar, mustard, sugar, and salt, and blend until smooth. With blender running, add vegetable oil in a slow, steady stream and blend until dressing is thick and smooth.
3. When ready to serve, pour enough dressing over lettuce to coat leaves well and toss. Serve any leftover dressing on side.

Summer Squash Soup
Steak with Pesto and Sour Cream
Marinated Zucchini Salad

Serve the pan-fried steak, topped with a spoonful of pesto and sour cream, and the marinated zucchini salad separately.

Sirloin steaks topped with sour cream and pesto are the entrée for this light summer dinner. Traditionally, Italian cooks use a mortar and pestle to grind the basil leaves, but a blender or food processor is faster. If you cannot find fresh basil, substitute dried basil and fresh parsley. The pesto will lack the intense taste and aroma of fresh basil, but the sauce will be delicious nonetheless.

WHAT TO DRINK

Choose a red wine with good body: a California Pinot Noir or a French Moulin à Vent.

SHOPPING LIST AND STAPLES

2 top sirloin steaks (beef top loin steaks), cut about ¾ inch thick (about 2 pounds total weight)
2 medium-size crookneck, or summer, squash
2 small zucchini (about 8 ounces total weight)
1 large tomato
1 medium-size carrot
1 medium-size onion
4 large cloves garlic
Large bunch fresh basil, or large bunch fresh parsley and 1 tablespoon dried basil

26

Small bunch fresh thyme, or ¼ teaspoon dried
Small bunch fresh marjoram, or ¼ teaspoon dried
Small bunch fresh rosemary, or ¼ teaspoon dried
Small bunch fresh dill, or ½ teaspoon dried
1½ cups milk
½ pint sour cream
4 tablespoons unsalted butter
¼ pound Parmesan or Romano cheese
1 pint plain yogurt
6-ounce can whole pitted black olives
⅔ cup olive oil
½ cup vegetable oil
⅓ cup white wine vinegar
¼ cup sugar
1 teaspoon instant chicken stock base
Salt and freshly ground pepper
3 tablespoons dry sherry

UTENSILS

Blender
Large skillet with cover
Large heavy-gauge skillet
Medium-size saucepan
Large bowl
Medium-size bowl
Small bowl
Salad bowl
9 x 9-inch metal pan, or pan with large surface area
Colander
Measuring cups and spoons
Chef's knife
Paring knife
Metal spatula
Grater
Vegetable peeler

START-TO-FINISH STEPS

1. Follow soup recipe steps 1 through 3.
2. While soup mixture is cooling, follow salad recipe steps 1 through 3. Put 4 soup bowls in refrigerator to chill.
3. Follow soup recipe step 4.
4. While soup is chilling, follow steak recipe step 1.
5. Follow soup recipe step 5 and serve.
6. Follow steak recipe steps 2 and 3, and serve with salad.

RECIPES

Summer Squash Soup

2 cups plain yogurt
1½ cups milk
2 tablespoons unsalted butter
2 medium-size crookneck squash, thinly sliced
Medium-size carrot, peeled and grated
Medium-size onion, peeled and minced
3 tablespoons sherry
¾ teaspoon chopped fresh dill, or ¼ teaspoon dried
1 teaspoon instant chicken stock base

1. In blender, combine yogurt and 1 cup milk, and blend 1 minute. Transfer mixture to medium-size bowl, cover, and refrigerate until needed.
2. In large skillet, melt butter over medium heat. Add squash, onion, carrot, and sherry. Cover pan and cook until squash is very tender, about 10 minutes.
3. Transfer vegetables to blender. Add dill and chicken stock base, and blend until mixture is smooth. Transfer mixture to large bowl and let cool about 10 minutes.
4. To vegetable mixture add 1½ cups of yogurt-milk mixture and the remaining milk. Stir until well blended and pour into metal pan with large surface area. Place in freezer to chill, about 15 minutes. Stir occasionally.
5. Serve in chilled bowls topped with yogurt-milk mixture.

Steak with Pesto and Sour Cream

Large bunch fresh basil, or large bunch fresh parsley combined with 1 tablespoon dried basil
1 cup freshly grated Parmesan or Romano cheese
⅔ cup olive oil
3 large cloves garlic, peeled
2 top sirloin steaks, ¾ inch thick (about 1 pound each)
Salt and freshly ground pepper
2 tablespoons unsalted butter
½ cup sour cream

1. Wash fresh basil or parsley and dry thoroughly. Discard thickest stems. You should have about 2 cups leaves. In blender, purée herbs, cheese, olive oil, and garlic.
2. Cut each steak in two and season with salt and pepper to taste. In large heavy-gauge skillet, melt butter over medium-high heat. Add steaks and cook 3 minutes per side for rare, 4 to 5 minutes per side for medium rare, and 7 to 8 minutes per side for well done.
3. Place a dollop of sour cream and another of pesto on each steak, and serve.

Marinated Zucchini Salad

2 cups ¼-inch-thick zucchini slices
½ cup vegetable oil
⅓ cup white wine vinegar
¼ cup sugar
Large clove garlic, peeled and minced
¾ teaspoon salt
¾ teaspoon chopped fresh thyme, or ¼ teaspoon dried
¾ teaspoon chopped fresh marjoram, or ¼ teaspoon dried
¾ teaspoon chopped fresh rosemary, or ¼ teaspoon dried
¾ teaspoon chopped fresh dill, or ¼ teaspoon dried
Large tomato, cut into wedges
½ cup whole pitted black olives, halved

1. In medium-size saucepan, bring 1 quart water to a boil. Add zucchini and simmer 2 minutes, or just until crisp-tender. Drain in colander, then pat dry.
2. In small bowl, combine oil, vinegar, sugar, garlic, salt, thyme, marjoram, rosemary, and dill.
3. Combine zucchini, tomato, and olives in salad bowl. Pour just enough dressing over salad to coat lightly and toss gently. Cover and refrigerate until ready to serve.

Jim Fobel

MENU 1 (Right)
Crisp-Fried Beef Cutlets with Taratoor Sauce
Sautéed Cherry Tomatoes
Sautéed Mushroom Medallions
Braised Belgian Endive

MENU 2
Stuffed Zucchini
Beef and Tomato Salad
Corn Wheels with Lemon-Pepper Butter
Herbed Garlic Bread

MENU 3
Peppered Rib Steaks
Grilled Onion Slices
Mashed Potatoes with Toasted Sesame Seeds
Green Beans with Bacon

J im Fobel believes that Americans are the finest cooks in the world, unafraid to combine ideas and techniques from different cuisines to forge a whole new way of eating. Much of his own approach comes from his international background. During his California childhood, he often visited his Japanese aunt in Hawaii. His family's next-door neighbor was a superlative Mexican cook. At a later date, his sister-in-law introduced him to Italian cuisine. Whether he is working in his New York test kitchen or preparing dinner for friends, he combines unorthodox flavors and textures.

Because his menus are so eclectic, he calls all three of them typically American. For Menu 1, the cooking technique for the beef is a traditional Italian method of preparing veal scallops: pounding the meat very thin, dredging it in bread crumbs, and frying it in oil and butter. But rather than sprinkle the beef cutlets with fresh lemon juice, as he might with veal, he spoons his variation of a zesty Middle Eastern *taratoor* sauce over them. Made from ground sesame seeds, lemon juice, and garlic, this sauce is sometimes served over vegetables or fish in Arab countries.

In Menu 2, he pairs a Mediterranean-style dish of zucchini stuffed with anchovies and black olives with a Mexican-influenced warm beef and tomato salad.

Menu 3 is another mingling of cuisines. The peppered rib steaks are accompanied by a Szechwan-style dish of dry fried green beans and mashed potatoes seasoned with Oriental sesame oil.

Grilled beef cutlets served with taratoor sauce and sprinkled with chives make a perfect dinner for guests. Mushroom medallions, braised endive, and sautéed cherry tomatoes accompany the meat. Serve extra sauce in a small pitcher.

28

Crisp-Fried Beef Cutlets with Taratoor Sauce
Sautéed Cherry Tomatoes / Sautéed Mushroom Medallions
Braised Belgian Endive

Pounding beef into thin cutlets, as Jim Fobel does for this menu, has several advantages: pounding tenderizes the beef so you can use less expensive cuts, if desired, and it reduces cooking time because the thin meat cooks quickly. The base for his *taratoor* sauce is *tahini*, a paste ground from untoasted sesame seeds, which is available in health food or specialty shops. Here the cook uses his own version of the traditional *taratoor* recipe.

Mild seasonings for the vegetable dishes offset the sharpness of the *taratoor* sauce. For the braised endive, Jim Fobel uses only a sprinkling of salt. Belgian endive, a member of the chicory family, comes in slender, compact heads resembling small unshucked ears of corn. Developed by a Belgian horticulturist, this costly crisp vegetable has a slightly bitter taste. Select heads that have firm pale stalks and leaves with pale yellow tips. Store endive in a plastic bag in your refrigerator and use within a few days.

For delicious mushrooms, buy those that are fresh-looking and unblemished, with tightly fitting caps that do not allow gills to show. Mushrooms will keep briefly in the refrigerator in a bowl covered with a damp towel, but they are best when used the day of purchase. Never wash or soak mushrooms; they absorb water and lose their flavor. Simply wipe them clean with a damp paper towel.

WHAT TO DRINK

To complement the piquant sauce, serve a varietal rosé from California. A lightly chilled Napa Gamay or Gamay Beaujolais would be a good alternative.

SHOPPING LIST AND STAPLES

4 boneless beef chuck, round, or sirloin steaks (about 1 pound total weight), cut ¼ inch thick, trimmed and pounded to ⅛ inch thick
1 pint cherry tomatoes
1 pound large firm mushrooms
4 small heads of Belgian endive (about ¾ pound total weight)
Large lemon
2 medium-size cloves garlic
Small bunch chives
2 eggs
1 stick unsalted butter
4 ounces Parmesan cheese

15-ounce can tahini (sesame seed paste)
¼ cup olive oil
½ to ¾ cup dried unflavored bread crumbs
Salt
Freshly ground pepper

UTENSILS

Food processor or blender
Large heavy-gauge skillet
Medium-size skillet
Medium-size saucepan with cover
Heatproof platter
2 heatproof plates
Cookie sheet or jelly roll pan
2 shallow bowls
Small bowl
Measuring cups and spoons
Chef's knife
Paring knife
Wooden spoon
Metal spatula
Large cake rack
Juicer (optional)
Metal tongs

START-TO-FINISH STEPS

1. Grate Parmesan cheese for beef cutlets recipe and mushrooms recipe.
2. Follow beef cutlets recipe steps 1 through 4.
3. Follow taratoor sauce recipe steps 1 though 3.
4. Follow tomatoes recipe step 1 and mushrooms recipe steps 1 and 2.
5. Follow beef cutlets recipe steps 5 and 6. As cutlets are frying, follow endive recipe steps 1 through 4.
6. Follow mushrooms recipe step 3 and endive recipe step 5.
7. Follow beef cutlets recipe step 7, cherry tomatoes recipe steps 2 and 3, mushrooms recipe step 4, endive recipe step 6, and serve.

RECIPES

Crisp-Fried Beef Cutlets

2 eggs
½ to ¾ cup dried unflavored bread crumbs

3 tablespoons freshly grated Parmesan cheese
1 teaspoon salt
½ teaspoon freshly ground pepper
4 boneless beef chuck, round, or sirloin steaks (about 1 pound total weight), cut ¼ inch thick, trimmed and pounded to ⅛ inch thick
2 tablespoons olive oil
2 tablespoons unsalted butter
Taratoor sauce (see following recipe)
1½ tablespoons snipped fresh chives

1. In shallow bowl, beat eggs with fork until well blended.
2. In second shallow bowl, combine bread crumbs, Parmesan cheese, salt, and pepper, and stir with fork until well blended.
3. Dip each cutlet in eggs and then in crumb mixture, patting meat to make crumbs adhere.
4. Place breaded cutlets on cake rack set on cookie sheet and refrigerate until ready to proceed.
5. Preheat oven to 140 degrees or lowest possible temperature.
6. In large skillet, heat oil over medium heat. Add butter and, when melted, increase heat to medium-high. When oil-butter mixture is almost smoking, place 2 cutlets in skillet, and fry until crisp and golden, about 2 to 3 minutes per side. Drain cutlets on paper towels and fry remaining cutlets in same manner. Transfer cutlets to heatproof platter and keep warm in preheated oven.
7. To serve, slice each cutlet into ½-inch-wide strips. Arrange strips on each plate to resemble cutlet before it was cut. Top cutlets with taratoor sauce, sprinkle with chopped chives, and serve remaining sauce separately.

Taratoor Sauce

2 medium-size cloves garlic
1 tablespoon olive oil
Large lemon
½ teaspoon salt
½ cup *tahini*

1. Peel and mince garlic. In medium-size skillet, heat olive oil over low heat. Add garlic and sauté about 1 minute. Do not let it brown.
2. Squeeze enough lemon to measure 3 tablespoons juice and remove pits. In food processor or blender, combine lemon juice, ½ cup cold water, and salt. Add sautéed garlic and oil in which it cooked. Process 30 seconds. Add *tahini* and process until smooth.
3. Transfer taratoor sauce to small bowl. Cover and set aside until ready to serve.

Sautéed Cherry Tomatoes

1 pint cherry tomatoes
1 tablespoon olive oil
Salt
Freshly ground pepper

1. Remove stems and wash and dry tomatoes.

2. In skillet used for endive, heat olive oil over medium heat. When oil is hot, add tomatoes and shake skillet to roll tomatoes and coat skins with oil. Sauté only 1 minute, so skins do not burst.
3. Sprinkle with salt and pepper to taste and serve immediately.

Sautéed Mushroom Medallions

1 pound large firm mushrooms
4 to 5 tablespoons unsalted butter
1 tablespoon freshly grated Parmesan cheese

1. Wipe mushrooms clean with damp paper towels.
2. Using mushroom stem as handle, slice each mushroom cap into ⅛-inch-thick medallions, or rounds, by slicing parallel to top. Reserve stem for another use. Cover mushrooms loosely and set aside until ready to proceed.
3. In skillet used for beef, melt butter over medium heat. Add mushrooms and quickly sauté over high heat, stirring and tossing them constantly until golden brown, about 4 to 5 minutes. Transfer to heatproof plate and keep warm in oven until ready to serve.
4. Divide among individual plates and sprinkle with grated Parmesan.

Braised Belgian Endive

4 small heads Belgian endive (about ¾ pound total weight)
½ teaspoon salt
1 tablespoon unsalted butter

1. Trim wilted leaves from endive and, using chef's knife, cut each in half lengthwise.
2. In medium-size saucepan, bring ½ cup water to a boil over high heat and then add salt.
3. Add endive, cut side up. Reduce heat to medium, partially cover pan, and braise endive 4 to 5 minutes, or just until tender when pierced with a fork. *Do not overcook.*
4. Using tongs, remove endive from pan and drain, cut side down, on paper towels. Set aside until ready to proceed.
5. Just before serving, melt butter over medium-low heat in skillet used for taratoor sauce. Place endive, cut side down, in skillet and cook over medium heat until golden brown, about 2 minutes. Transfer to heatproof plate and keep warm in oven until ready to serve.
6. Divide among individual plates and set cut side up.

LEFTOVER SUGGESTION

Any leftover cutlets provide the makings for a wonderful sandwich. Warm the cutlets in a small, ungreased skillet over low heat, about 5 minutes. Then cut them into 1-inch squares, toss with shredded Romaine lettuce and chopped tomatoes, and stuff into heated pita-bread pockets. Top the filling with taratoor sauce and toasted sesame seeds.

Stuffed Zucchini
Beef and Tomato Salad/Corn Wheels with Lemon-Pepper Butter
Herbed Garlic Bread

The main-course salad of stir-fried strips of flank steak and cut-up ripe tomatoes may be eaten warm or chilled. To keep the steak strips juicy and tender, stir fry them quickly. For the best flavor, use vine-ripened tomatoes or, if none are available, substitute drained canned tomatoes.

The zucchini in the appetizer are stuffed with a mixture of anchovies, olives, lemon juice, and capers. This dish can be served warm, at room temperature, or chilled. Zucchini are readily available year-round but are most plentiful in the summer. Select firm ones and store them in a plastic bag in the refrigerator. Tart capers, the small unopened

This colorful meal of stuffed zucchini, warm beef and tomato salad garnished with sour cream, garlic bread, and corn "wheels" has both Mediterranean and Mexican touches.

buds of a Mediterranean bush, usually come vinegar-packed in jars. They are available in most supermarkets and in Italian groceries. They keep for months in the refrigerator.

To complete this eclectic menu, Jim Fobel calls for corn wheels with lemon-pepper butter, which is a Mexican-style dish, and an Italian-inspired herbed garlic bread.

WHAT TO DRINK

Corn's natural sweetness can sometimes overwhelm the taste of wine. However, the combination of fresh, summery ingredients here calls for a young wine, such as a French Beaujolais or a California Gamay Beaujolais.

SHOPPING LIST AND STAPLES

1 pound beef flank steak (trimmed weight)
2 medium-size zucchini (about 1 pound total weight)
3 medium-size ripe tomatoes (about 1 pound total weight)
4 medium-size ears of corn
Small head Romaine lettuce
1 bunch scallions
2 lemons
1 clove garlic
Medium-size bunch fresh parsley
Small bunch fresh oregano or 2 teaspoons dried
1 tablespoon fresh basil or 1 teaspoon dried
½ pint sour cream
1 stick unsalted butter
¼ pound sharp Cheddar cheese
2-ounce can flat anchovy fillets
6-ounce can pitted black olives
3½-ounce jar capers
3 tablespoons olive oil
1 loaf Italian bread (about 14 inches long)
½ cup unseasoned bread crumbs
1 tablespoon sugar
1 teaspoon paprika (optional)
Salt
Freshly ground pepper

UTENSILS

Large heavy-gauge skillet or wok
Large saucepan with cover
2 small saucepans
Small broiler pan
Serving platter
Medium-size bowl
Small bowl
Colander
Salad spinner (optional)
Measuring cups and spoons
Chef's knife or cleaver
Bread knife
Paring knife
Large slotted spoon (optional)
Wooden spoon
Metal spatula
Chinese wok spatulas or 2 wooden spoons

START-TO-FINISH STEPS

1. For beef recipe, remove sour cream from refrigerator to bring to room temperature.
2. Follow zucchini recipe step 1. While heating water, wash and trim scallions and slice into thin rounds for zucchini

and beef recipes. Wash and finely chop parsley for beef recipe and for zucchini recipe, if using.

3. Follow zucchini recipe steps 2 through 4.

4. While zucchini is cooking, follow beef recipe step 1.

5. While zucchini is cooling, follow beef recipe steps 2 and 3.

6. Follow corn recipe step 1.

7. While heating water, follow zucchini recipe steps 5 through 7 and serve. (Leave broiler on for garlic bread.)

8. Follow corn recipe step 2. While corn is cooking, follow garlic bread recipe steps 1 and 2, and corn recipe step 3.

9. Follow beef recipe step 4 and corn recipe step 4.

10. Follow garlic bread recipe step 3, corn recipe step 5, beef recipe step 5, and serve.

RECIPES

Stuffed Zucchini

½ teaspoon salt
6 flat anchovy fillets
2 tablespoons capers
½ cup pitted black olives
1 lemon
2 medium-size zucchini (about 1 pound total weight)
½ cup unseasoned bread crumbs
2 tablespoons olive oil
¼ cup thinly sliced scallions
¼ teaspoon freshly ground pepper
2 tablespoons chopped parsley for garnish (optional)

1. In large covered saucepan, bring 3 quarts water and salt to a boil over high heat.

2. Rinse anchovies and pat dry. Chop anchovies, capers, and olives, and combine in medium-size bowl. Squeeze enough lemon to measure 1 tablespoon juice, remove pits, and add to bowl. Set aside.

3. Place broiler shelf 5 to 6 inches from heat source and preheat broiler.

4. Wash and trim zucchini and halve lengthwise. Drop into boiling water, return to a boil, and cook 4 minutes, uncovered. Using slotted spoon, transfer zucchini to colander and rinse under cold running water until cool enough to handle. Reserve hot cooking water for corn recipe.

5. For stuffing, add bread crumbs, olive oil, scallions, and pepper to anchovy mixture and, using wooden spoon, stir to combine.

6. Using spoon, scoop out pulp from each zucchini half, leaving a shell about ¼ inch thick. Chop 3 tablespoons of pulp and add to stuffing mixture. Discard remaining pulp. Using paper towels, pat inside of zucchini shells dry and place zucchini, cut side up, in small broiler pan. Divide stuffing among 4 halves; do not pack down, but mound slightly.

7. Place pan on broiler shelf and broil 3 to 5 minutes, or until filling has browned. Transfer zucchini to serving platter and garnish with chopped parsley, if desired.

Beef and Tomato Salad

4 Romaine lettuce leaves
3 medium-size ripe tomatoes (about 1 pound total weight)
1 pound beef flank steak (trimmed weight)
1 tablespoon olive oil
1 tablespoon chopped fresh basil or 1 teaspoon dried, crumbled
½ cup sour cream, at room temperature
¾ cup thinly sliced scallions
½ cup finely chopped parsley
Salt
Freshly ground pepper

1. Wash lettuce leaves and dry in salad spinner or pat dry with paper towels. Line serving platter with leaves.

2. Wash, dry, halve, and seed tomatoes. Cut into ½-inch dice. Set aside in small bowl.

3. With chef's knife, cut steak lengthwise, with grain, into long strips about 2 inches wide. Cut strips, across grain, into ⅛-inch-wide slices.

4. In large heavy-gauge skillet or wok, heat oil over medium-high heat until almost smoking. Add beef and basil and, using Chinese wok spatulas or 2 wooden spoons, stir fry just until meat loses pink color, about 2 minutes. Add tomatoes and stir fry until they are just warm, about 1 minute. Transfer mixture to serving platter lined with lettuce leaves.

5. Top with sour cream, scallions, and parsley. Season with salt and pepper to taste, and toss gently to combine.

Corn Wheels with Lemon-Pepper Butter

4 medium-size ears of corn
1 tablespoon sugar
4 tablespoons unsalted butter
1 lemon
½ teaspoon freshly ground pepper

1. Reheat water used for zucchini recipe and bring to a boil. Shuck corn and trim ends, if necessary.
2. Add sugar and corn to boiling water. Cover pan and return to a boil. Remove pan from heat and set aside, covered, 5 minutes.
3. Melt butter in small saucepan. Squeeze lemon and remove pits. Add lemon juice and pepper to melted butter, and stir to combine.
4. With tongs, remove corn and hold over pan to drain. With chef's knife or cleaver, cut each ear into four 2-inch wheels.
5. Transfer corn to serving platter and drizzle with lemon-pepper butter.

Herbed Garlic Bread

4 tablespoons unsalted butter
1 clove garlic
¼ pound sharp Cheddar cheese
1 loaf Italian bread (about 14 inches long)
1 tablespoon plus 1 teaspoon chopped fresh oregano
    or 2 teaspoons dried
1 teaspoon paprika (optional)

1. Melt butter in small saucepan. Peel and mince garlic. Coarsely grate enough cheese to measure ½ cup.
2. Using bread knife, cut bread in half lengthwise. Drizzle butter evenly over cut surface of bread. Sprinkle with garlic, oregano, and cheese. If desired, sprinkle paprika in evenly spaced diagonal lines over cheese.
3. Place bread under broiler 1 to 2 minutes, until cheese is melted and bread is golden brown. Cut into slices and serve.

ADDED TOUCH

You can bake this cake the day before you serve it, then assemble it at the last moment.

Peaches-and-Cream Cake

4 tablespoons unsalted butter (approximately)
⅔ cup sugar
5 eggs, at room temperature
1 teaspoon vanilla extract
1 cup plus 2 tablespoons all-purpose flour
2 cups heavy cream, plus ½ cup for garnish, chilled
¾ cup sifted confectioners' sugar
½ teaspoon almond extract

5 medium-size ripe freestone peaches
    (about 1¼ pounds total weight), plus 1 additional
    for garnish (optional)
¾ cup peach preserves

1. Chill bowl and beaters. Grease two 8-inch round cake pans with butter, dust with 2 tablespoons flour, and tap out excess. Preheat oven to 350 degrees. In small saucepan, melt 3 tablespoons butter over low heat without browning.
2. Choose a stainless steel bowl that will fit into or over a large saucepan. Add just enough water to pan to bring water level about 1 inch below bottom of bowl. Bring water to a simmer over medium heat. Off heat, combine sugar and eggs in bowl and whisk until thoroughly blended. Place bowl over pan and continue whisking just until mixture is warm. Remove bowl and beat mixture at high speed 2 minutes. Then, beat at moderate speed until mixture is pale yellow, thick, and tripled in volume, about 5 minutes. It should be cool and form a ribbon when beaters are lifted. Stir in vanilla extract.
3. Working quickly, fold in remaining flour with rubber spatula, one third at a time. Fold in melted butter. Divide batter evenly between cake pans, smooth tops with rubber spatula, and place pans in oven. Bake until puffed and light golden brown, 25 to 30 minutes. Top will spring back when touched and edge will begin to pull away from pan. Cool 10 minutes, then invert onto rack and cool completely. (If preparing in advance, wrap in plastic and refrigerate.)
4. For filling, using chilled beaters and bowl, beat 2 cups cream at high speed until soft peaks form. Decrease speed to medium and gradually add confectioners' sugar, continuing to beat until stiff peaks form. Stir in almond extract. Cover and refrigerate until needed.
5. Peel 5 peaches and cut into ½ inch-thick slices.
6. With long serrated knife, cut each cake into 2 layers.
7. Place strainer over small saucepan and, using back of wooden spoon, force through peach preserves. Bring to a boil, over medium heat, stirring until liquid.
8. Place one bottom layer on serving plate. In order, cover with one third each of hot peach glaze, peach slices, and whipped cream. Repeat process with next 2 layers. If glaze cools, reheat it until liquid, adding a few drops water if necessary. Add top layer of cake. Cover and chill until ready to serve.
9. Before serving, beat remaining cream and cut remaining peach into 8 even slices for garnish, if desired.

Peppered Rib Steaks / Grilled Onion Slices
Mashed Potatoes with Toasted Sesame Seeds
Green Beans with Bacon

Serve the peppered rib steaks with their brandy and cream sauce, the grilled onions, and the sesame-flavored mashed potatoes on individual dinner plates. The stir-fried green beans with bacon make a pleasing side dish.

The boneless peppered rib steaks resemble the French *steak au poivre*, which customarily are made with coarsely ground black pepper and Cognac. For this version, the cook adds heavy cream to the Cognac and pan juices.

The mashed potatoes are seasoned with Oriental sesame oil—a highly aromatic oil that is used for flavoring, not for cooking. Always buy a Japanese or Chinese brand; the cold-pressed health food and Middle Eastern oils lack the rich, nutty taste of the Far Eastern varieties.

WHAT TO DRINK

For this red-wine menu, choose a good-quality California Cabernet Sauvignon or Zinfandel, a good village Burgundy, or a Barolo from Italy's Piedmont area.

SHOPPING LIST AND STAPLES

4 boneless beef rib steaks (8 ounces each), cut about
   ¾ inch thick
6 slices bacon (about ¼ pound total weight)
1 pound medium-size green beans
5 medium-size baking potatoes (about 2 pounds total
   weight)
2 medium-size onions
Small bunch fresh rosemary, or 2 teaspoons dried
Small bunch fresh parsley (optional)
⅓ cup milk
½ pint heavy cream
3 tablespoons unsalted butter
3 tablespoons olive oil
2 tablespoons Oriental sesame oil
2 tablespoons cider vinegar
4 teaspoons sesame seeds
2 teaspoons sugar
Salt and freshly ground pepper
¼ cup Cognac

UTENSILS

2 large heavy-gauge skillets, one non-aluminum
Small heavy-gauge skillet or saucepan
Large saucepan with cover
Griddle or large heavy-gauge skillet
Heatproof platter
Ovenproof bowl

Colander
Measuring cups and spoons
Chef's knife
Paring knife
Wooden spoon
Slotted spoon
Metal spatula
Potato masher or electric mixer
Metal tongs

START-TO-FINISH STEPS

1. Follow steaks recipe step 1 and potatoes recipe steps 1 through 3.
2. While potatoes are cooking, preheat oven to 200 degrees and follow green beans recipe steps 1 through 3, and onions recipe step 1.
3. Follow steaks recipe step 2 and onions recipe step 2.
4. While steaks and onions are cooking, follow potatoes recipe step 4.
5. Follow steaks recipe step 3. While sauce is thickening, follow green beans recipe step 4 and onions recipe step 3.
6. Follow steaks recipe step 4, potatoes recipe step 5, and serve with green beans and onions.

RECIPES

Peppered Rib Steaks

4 boneless beef rib steaks (8 ounces each), cut about
   ¾ inch thick
6 teaspoons coarsely ground pepper
2 tablespoons olive oil
¼ cup Cognac
¾ cup heavy cream
¼ teaspoon salt
2 tablespoons chopped fresh parsley (optional)

1. Trim away and discard any excess fat from steaks. Rub ½ teaspoon pepper into each steak, coating both sides.
2. In large heavy-gauge skillet, heat 1 tablespoon oil over medium-high heat. Cook 2 steaks, turning with tongs several times, about 2 to 3 minutes per side for rare, 3 to 4 minutes per side for medium rare, or 5 to 7 minutes per side for well done. To test for doneness, cut into center of steak and check color. Transfer steaks to heatproof platter and keep warm in oven. If necessary, add second tablespoon olive oil, and repeat process with remaining steaks.
3. Pour Cognac into skillet and, stirring continuously, scrape up any brown bits from bottom of pan. Stir in remaining 4 teaspoons pepper and cream. Reduce heat to medium and cook about 3 minutes, until sauce is just thickened. Add salt to taste.
4. Transfer steaks to individual plates. Spoon a little sauce over each and garnish with chopped parsley, if desired.

Grilled Onion Slices

2 medium-size onions
1 tablespoon olive oil

1 tablespoon minced fresh rosemary or 2 teaspoons dried
Salt and freshly ground pepper

1. Peel onions and cut crosswise into slices just slightly thicker than ¼ inch.
2. Place ungreased griddle or large heavy-gauge skillet over medium heat. Add onion slices in a single layer. Cook, frequently pressing down with spatula and turning carefully several times, until slices are deep brown and lightly charred, about 10 minutes.
3. Drizzle slices with olive oil and sprinkle with rosemary. Continue cooking, turning several times with spatula, until onions are soft and fragrant, about 2 minutes. If necessary, reduce heat slightly to prevent smoking. Sprinkle with salt and pepper to taste.

Mashed Potatoes with Toasted Sesame Seeds

4 teaspoons sesame seeds
5 medium-size baking potatoes
1 teaspoon salt
3 tablespoons unsalted butter
⅓ cup milk
2 tablespoons Oriental sesame oil

1. In large covered saucepan, bring 1½ quarts water to a simmer over high heat.
2. In small heavy-gauge skillet or saucepan, toast sesame seeds over medium heat, stirring or tossing constantly until golden brown, about 2 minutes.
3. Peel potatoes and cut into 1½-inch chunks. Add salt and potatoes to pan, partially cover and simmer until potatoes are tender when pierced with fork, 10 to 15 minutes.
4. Drain potatoes thoroughly and return to pan. Add butter, milk, and sesame oil. Using potato masher or electric mixer, mash or beat potatoes until smooth. If dry, beat in a little more milk. Transfer potatoes to ovenproof bowl and keep warm in oven.
5. Remove potatoes from oven and divide equally among 4 plates. Sprinkle each portion with toasted sesame seeds.

Green Beans with Bacon

6 slices bacon (about ¼ pound total weight), chilled
1 pound medium-size green beans
2 teaspoons sugar
2 tablespoons cider vinegar
¼ teaspoon salt

1. Using chef's knife, cut through stacked bacon slices to make ¼-inch squares.
2. In large heavy-gauge skillet, cook bacon, stirring frequently, over medium-high heat until crisp and golden brown, about 5 minutes. With slotted spoon, transfer bacon to paper towels. Pour off all but 1 tablespoon fat.
3. While bacon is frying, wash green beans and pat dry. Top and tail beans and cut into 1½-inch lengths.
4. Add green beans to skillet and stir fry over medium heat until blistered and tender, 3 to 4 minutes. Stir in sugar and remove skillet from heat. Stir in vinegar and salt. Add bacon and toss to combine. Serve hot or warm.

Diana Sturgis

Diana Sturgis, who now lives in New York, comments on her native land: "My area of south Wales was mountainous and rural, and we had few fresh foods or sophisticated ingredients." Of necessity, housewives wasted nothing edible and had to create simple dishes using only a few staples. The chef's commitment to beautiful meals and fresh produce derives in part from the years in which she saw the drab food of her Welsh childhood transformed by her mother's ability to turn commonplace ingredients into something special.

She is fascinated by the techniques and chemistry of cooking, and she believes that understanding these basic principles contributes to the perfection of a meal. For example, in both Menu 1 and Menu 3, she calls for marinating the meat before cooking it, which both flavors and tenderizes it. In Menu 1, this process is short because the beef and veal are high-quality and are cut into cubes. In Menu 3, on the other hand, the meat, a thick steak, requires longer marinating, ideally overnight, to tenderize it and to absorb all the flavors in the marinade: wine, garlic, mustard, and herbs.

Menu 2 is a good example of simple ingredients combined tastefully and decoratively: browned veal rib chops with a cream sauce flavored with Cognac and tarragon, steamed green beans, and sautéed mushrooms.

Skewered beef and veal cubes on a bed of rice with raisins, a dish of corn flavored with paprika and lime juice, and broiled eggplant halves make a informal meal, perfect for family or friends. For extra color, garnish the corn with slices of fresh lime.

39

Veal, Beef, and Eggplant Brochettes
Raisin Rice
Tangy Corn

Cubes of veal and beef, threaded on skewers and broiled, are the focal point of this summer meal. The meat marinade includes powdered cumin. This amber spice, an important seasoning in Asian, Middle Eastern, and Mexican recipes, is highly aromatic and particularly good with beef. Since freshly ground cumin tastes best, buy the whole seeds from your supermarket spice section, and pulverize what you need in a blender or a mortar and pestle.

The eggplants are also skewered and broiled. Baby eggplants have fewer seeds than the large varieties and they are less likely to be bitter. Allow one per serving. Select firm eggplants with shiny purple skins. Since the skin is tender, you do not need to pare it. Stored in a plastic bag, eggplants keep for up to one week in the refrigerator.

WHAT TO DRINK
Choose a red wine of medium body and bright flavor, either a California Merlot or a Chianti Classico.

SHOPPING LIST AND STAPLES
¾ pound boneless veal leg, cut ¾ inch thick
¾ pound boneless top sirloin, cut ¾ inch thick
4 baby eggplants (about 1 pound total weight)
4 ears fresh corn, or two 10-ounce frozen packages
1 small onion
3 limes
3 tablespoons unsalted butter
1¾ cups chicken stock, preferably homemade (see page 13), or canned (optional)
⅓ cup corn oil
1 cup long-grain white rice
⅓ cup raisins (golden or dark)
¼ teaspoon ground cumin
1 teaspoon paprika
Salt and freshly ground pepper

UTENSILS
Medium-size heavy-gauge saucepan with cover
Medium-size saucepan with cover
Small saucepan (optional)
Broiler pan
Medium-size bowl
Colander
Fine mesh sieve or strainer
Measuring cups and spoons
Chef's knife
Paring knife
Wooden spoon
Whisk
8 long metal skewers
Pastry brush

START-TO-FINISH STEPS
1. Squeeze lime for corn and brochettes recipes and mince onion for brochettes recipe.
2. Follow brochettes recipe steps 1 and 2.
3. Follow corn recipe step 1.
4. Follow rice recipe steps 1 through 3.
5. While rice is cooking, follow brochettes recipe steps 3 through 5.
6. While meat is broiling, follow corn recipe step 2.
7. Just before meat is done, follow rice recipe step 4.
8. Follow brochettes recipe step 6 and serve with corn.

RECIPES
Veal, Beef, and Eggplant Brochettes

⅓ cup corn oil
1 tablespoon fresh lime juice
¼ teaspoon ground cumin
½ teaspoon freshly ground pepper
½ cup minced onion
¾ pound boneless veal leg, cut ¾ inch thick
¾ pound boneless top sirloin, cut ¾ inch thick
4 baby eggplants (about 1 pound total weight)
¾ teaspoon salt

1. In medium-size bowl, combine ¼ cup oil with lime juice, ground cumin, and ¼ teaspoon pepper, and whisk until blended. Add minced onion and stir to combine.
2. Cut veal and beef into 1- to 1½-inch-wide slices and add to marinade. Stir to coat meat and set aside to marinate 30 minutes.
3. Preheat broiler. Rinse eggplants and dry with paper towels, trim off stems, and cut in half lengthwise. Pierce cut side all over with fork and thread each half lengthwise, through rounded portion, onto 4 metal skewers (see diagram). Brush with remaining oil and sprinkle with remaining black pepper and ¼ teaspoon salt.

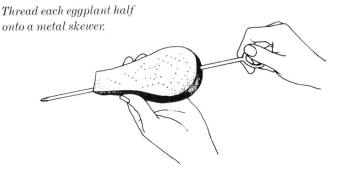

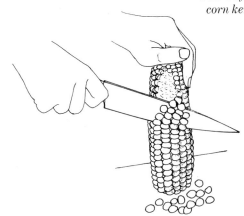

4. With slotted spoon, remove meat from marinade and, if desired, reserve marinade to be served as a sauce. Thread veal and beef alternately onto remaining 4 skewers and sprinkle meat with remaining salt.

5. Place skewers on broiler pan and place in preheated broiler, about 4 inches from heat source. Cook, turning to brown on all sides, about 10 minutes. Do not baste.

6. Arrange meat skewers on bed of raisin rice. Remove eggplant from skewers and transfer to serving platter. If desired, pour marinade into small saucepan and bring to a boil over medium heat. Reduce heat and simmer 1 minute. Transfer to sauce boat and serve separately.

Raisin Rice

1 cup long-grain white rice
1¾ cups chicken stock or water
⅓ cup raisins (golden or dark)
¼ teaspoon salt (optional)
1 tablespoon unsalted butter

1. In fine mesh sieve, rinse rice under cold running water.

2. In medium-size heavy-gauge saucepan, combine rice with chicken stock or water and bring to a boil over medium heat. (If you are using water, add salt at this point).

3. Stir in raisins. Cover and turn heat as low as possible. Cook, without lifting cover, 17 minutes, then turn off heat. Rice will keep hot for at least 30 minutes.

4. Before serving, remove cover, add butter, and fluff rice with fork. Transfer to serving platter and form bed for brochettes.

Tangy Corn

4 ears fresh corn or 3 cups frozen
2 tablespoons lime juice
2 tablespoons unsalted butter, melted
¼ teaspoon salt (optional)
1 teaspoon paprika
Freshly ground pepper

1. If using fresh corn, remove husks and silk. With chef's knife, trim off stem end so upended ears will sit flat on cutting surface. Holding 1 ear of corn upright, press base against table and, with chef's knife, cut off kernels by pressing blade against cob and slicing downward. Turn corn and repeat process until all kernels are removed. Repeat process for remaining ears.

2. In medium-size saucepan, combine kernels with 1 cup

water. Bring to a boil, cover, and simmer over medium heat about 5 minutes, or until tender. Cooking time will depend on age of corn. If using frozen corn, cook according to package instructions. Drain kernels in colander and transfer to serving bowl. Add lime juice, butter, salt, paprika, and pepper and toss to combine.

ADDED TOUCH

When you are preparing this rich chocolaty dessert, take care to heat the small pieces of chocolate just until they melt. Overheating makes the chocolate granular.

Mocha Mousse

4 ounces bittersweet chocolate
4 tablespoons coffee liqueur, such as Tia Maria
2 teaspoons instant coffee (not freeze dried)
2 tablespoons unsalted butter
2 eggs
2 tablespoons sugar
½ cup heavy cream
4 coffee beans (optional)

1. Chill 4 stemmed glasses. Break chocolate into small pieces. In top of double boiler, combine chocolate, liqueur, 1 teaspoon coffee powder, and butter. Set over—not in—simmering water until chocolate begins to melt, about 4 minutes. While chocolate is melting, separate eggs.

2. Remove chocolate mixture from heat and, with wooden spoon, stir until smooth. Add egg yolks to chocolate mixture and beat until thoroughly combined.

3. In deep bowl, beat egg whites until soft peaks form, about 3 to 4 minutes. Gradually beat in sugar and beat until mixture is stiff but not dry.

4. In small bowl, with same beaters, beat cream until thick and approximately doubled in volume.

5. Add three quarters of whipped cream to chocolate mixture and stir to combine.

6. With rubber spatula, gently fold in egg whites just until no streaks of white remain.

7. Spoon mixture into stemmed glasses. Top each glass with a portion of remaining whipped cream and a coffee bean. Chill until ready to serve.

Veal Chops with Tarragon Sauce
Green Beans and Sautéed Mushrooms

Pepper-coated veal chops and a side dish of green beans and sautéed mushrooms make a simple yet elegant dinner or lunch.

Rib veal chops have slightly less meat than the loin but are equally tender. Each chop should weigh about ten ounces before being boned, and about seven ounces after. Ask the butcher to bone the chops, or bone them at home. Stand the chop upright with the bone perpendicular to the cutting surface and slice downward, as close to the bone as possible, carving the meat out in one piece.

WHAT TO DRINK

This adaptation of a French dish should have a French wine. First choice would be a St. Julien or a St. Emilion.

SHOPPING LIST AND STAPLES

4 boned veal rib chops (each about 7 ounces), with "tail" attached
1 pound mushrooms
1 pound green beans or two 10-ounce packages frozen
Large clove garlic
1 lemon
Small bunch fresh tarragon or ½ teaspoon dried
½ pint heavy cream
5 tablespoons unsalted butter (approximately)
¾ cup chicken stock, preferably homemade (see page 13), or canned
1 teaspoon Dijon mustard
Salt and freshly ground pepper
¼ cup brandy, preferably Cognac

UTENSILS

Large heavy-gauge skillet
Medium-size skillet
Medium-size saucepan with cover
Small saucepan
Vegetable steamer
Heatproof platter
Large bowl
Small bowl
Fine mesh sieve or strainer
Measuring cups and spoons
Chef's knife
Paring knife
Wooden spoon
Metal spatula
8 rounded wooden toothpicks

START-TO-FINISH STEPS

1. Follow veal recipe steps 1 through 3.
2. Follow green beans recipe steps 1 and 2.
3. Follow veal recipe steps 4 through 6.
4. Follow green beans recipe steps 3 and 4.
5. Follow veal recipe step 7.
6. Follow green beans recipe step 5 and veal recipe step 8.
7. Serve veal with green beans and mushrooms.

RECIPES

Veal Chops with Tarragon Sauce

4 boned veal rib chops with "tail" attached
Freshly ground pepper
3 tablespoons unsalted butter
Large clove garlic
¾ cup chicken stock
¼ cup brandy, preferably Cognac
1½ teaspoons chopped fresh tarragon or ½ teaspoon dried
½ cup heavy cream
Salt

1. In small saucepan, melt butter over very low heat. Turn off heat and skim off foam. Carefully pour off golden clarified butter and reserve. Discard residue.
2. Preheat oven to 200 degrees. Form each chop into a cutlet by attaching the long fatty tail to the lean section with 2 rounded wooden toothpicks. (Do not pull or stretch meat.) Score fatty edge at ½-inch intervals. Sprinkle both sides of meat with pepper.
3. In large heavy-gauge skillet, heat clarified butter over medium heat. Add garlic, reduce heat to low, and cook 2 minutes. Do not let garlic brown. Discard garlic.
4. Increase heat to high, add chops, and brown quickly on both sides. Reduce heat to medium and cook, turning once, 15 minutes.
5. Transfer chops to platter, cover loosely with foil, and keep warm in oven.
6. Pour drippings from veal into medium-size skillet and reserve for green beans.
7. For sauce, add stock, brandy, and tarragon to skillet. Over high heat, deglaze pan by scraping up browned bits from bottom. Add cream and, over medium heat, reduce sauce to ¾ cup, about 5 minutes. Add salt and pepper to taste and put sauce through fine strainer. Keep warm.
8. Spoon sauce onto plates and top each with veal chop.

Green Beans and Sautéed Mushrooms

Pan drippings from veal chops
1 or 2 tablespoons unsalted butter, if needed
1 pound mushrooms
1 pound green beans or two 10-ounce packages frozen
1 teaspoon Dijon mustard
1½ tablespoons lemon juice
Salt and freshly ground pepper

1. In medium-size covered saucepan, bring water to a boil. Clean mushrooms and cut into ¼-inch slices.
2. Top, tail, and wash green beans.
3. In medium-size skillet, heat drippings from veal chops over medium heat, add mushrooms, and sauté until browned, 8 to 10 minutes. Add butter, if needed.
4. Place steamer in saucepan. Add beans, cover pan, and steam just until crisp-tender, about 6 minutes.
5. In large bowl, combine beans and mushrooms. In small bowl, combine mustard and lemon juice. Add to vegetables with salt and pepper to taste, and toss to combine.

London Broil with Red Wine Marinade
Broiled Tomatoes / Orzo with Parmesan
Avocado Salad

Slices of steak garnished with watercress, a broiled tomato half sprinkled with Parmesan cheese, and a serving of orzo is a delicious hearty meal that looks good in any table setting.

Diana Sturgis prepares boneless beef chuck shoulder (clod) steaks for her London broil. Several other cuts of meat are commonly used for London broil, including beef round top round steak, flank steak, and beef plate skirt steak. Meat cooked according to the London broil method is first marinated for several hours to tenderize it and then broiled.

To absorb the meat juices the steak is served with orzo, a pasta favored by Greeks. Orzo looks like rice, but the cooked grains are twice as large as long-grain rice.

WHAT TO DRINK

To complement the meat, buy a full-bodied red wine—a California Cabernet Sauvignon or a St. Estèphe.

SHOPPING LIST AND STAPLES

1¾ pounds trimmed boneless beef chuck shoulder steak (clod), cut 1¼ inches thick
2 small bunches watercress
1 head Boston or butter lettuce
2 ripe avocados
Small cucumber
4 firm ripe tomatoes (about 1 pound total weight)
Large clove garlic
2 tablespoons plus 1 teaspoon unsalted butter
¼ pound Parmesan cheese
4 tablespoons vegetable oil
2 tablespoons safflower oil
2 tablespoons olive oil
1½ teaspoons Dijon mustard
1½ tablespoons white wine vinegar
8 ounces orzo pasta
⅛ teaspoon dried thyme
Salt and freshly ground pepper
½ cup dry red wine, preferably Burgundy

UTENSILS

Large saucepan with cover
Broiler pan
13 x 9 x 2-inch glass baking dish
Serving platter
Plate
Large bowl
2 medium-size bowls

Strainer
Salad spinner (optional)
Measuring cups and spoons
Chef's knife
Paring knife
Grater
Whisk
Metal tongs
Vegetable peeler

START-TO-FINISH STEPS

The night before or 1½ hours ahead: Follow London broil recipe steps 1 and 2.

1. Follow London broil recipe step 3 and orzo recipe step 1.
2. While broiler and water are heating, grate Parmesan for tomatoes recipe, if using, and for orzo recipe.
3. Follow London broil recipe step 4 and salad recipe steps 1 through 3.
4. Follow London broil recipe step 5.
5. While meat is broiling, follow salad recipe step 4 and tomatoes recipe steps 1 and 2.
6. Follow London broil recipe step 6, tomatoes recipe step 3, and orzo recipe step 2.
7. Follow London broil recipe step 7, orzo recipe step 3, and serve with tomatoes and salad.

RECIPES

London Broil with Red Wine Marinade

½ cup dry red wine, preferably Burgundy
Large clove garlic, crushed
¼ cup vegetable oil
¼ teaspoon freshly ground pepper
½ teaspoon Dijon mustard
⅛ teaspoon dried thyme
1¾ pounds trimmed boneless beef chuck shoulder steak
    (clod), cut 1¼ inches thick
Small bunch of watercress

1. For marinade, combine wine, garlic, oil, pepper, mustard and thyme in medium-size bowl.
2. With fork, pierce meat deeply about a dozen times on both sides. Place meat in glass baking dish just large enough to hold it. Pour marinade over meat and turn once to coat. Cover and refrigerate 1 hour or overnight, turning meat once or twice.
3. Set broiler rack about 4 inches from heat source and preheat broiler.
4. Wash watercress and dry in salad spinner or pat dry with paper towels.
5. Remove meat from marinade and pat dry with paper towels. Warm serving platter under hot running water. Place meat in broiler pan and broil 6 minutes for rare, 8 minutes for medium rare, 10 minutes for medium, or 12 minutes for well done. Using metal tongs, turn meat once, being careful not to pierce it. Dry platter.
6. Transfer meat to warmed platter and allow to rest 10

minutes. Leave broiler on for tomatoes recipe.
7. Cut meat across grain into slices about ¼ inch thick. Garnish with sprigs of watercress.

Broiled Tomatoes

4 firm ripe tomatoes (about 1 pound total weight)
Salt and freshly ground pepper
1 tablespoon freshly grated Parmesan cheese (optional)
1 tablespoon plus 1 teaspoon unsalted butter

1. Wash and halve tomatoes. Place on broiler pan.
2. Sprinkle tomatoes with salt and pepper to taste and, if desired, with Parmesan cheese. Top each half with ½ teaspoon butter.
3. Place broiler pan about 4 inches from heat source. Broil tomatoes until nicely browned on top, about 10 minutes.

Orzo with Parmesan

Salt
1 cup orzo pasta
1 tablespoon unsalted butter
¼ cup freshly grated Parmesan cheese
Freshly ground black pepper

1. In large covered saucepan, bring 2 quarts lightly salted water to a boil.
2. Add orzo and cook, uncovered, at a rolling boil until *al dente*, about 9 to 10 minutes.
3. Using strainer, drain pasta well over medium-size bowl. Dry bowl. Transfer orzo to warmed bowl, add butter and cheese, and toss to coat evenly. Add salt and pepper to taste, and serve.

Avocado Salad

Small bunch watercress
1 head Boston or butter lettuce
2 tablespoons safflower oil
2 tablespoons olive oil
1½ tablespoons white wine vinegar
1 teaspoon Dijon mustard
½ teaspoon salt
¼ teaspoon freshly ground pepper
Small cucumber
2 ripe avocados

1. Remove stems from watercress and separate into small sprigs. Wash watercress and lettuce and dry in salad spinner or pat dry with paper towels.
2. In large bowl, combine oils, vinegar, mustard, and salt and pepper, whisking until thoroughly blended.
3. Line 4 salad bowls with lettuce leaves. Place watercress on plate and transfer it and bowls to refrigerator to chill.
4. Peel cucumber and slice thinly. Halve avocados lengthwise, twist apart gently, and remove pits. Peel, slice into wedges, and cut into ¾-inch chunks. Add to bowl with dressing and toss gently to coat. Add cucumber slices and watercress sprigs, and turn into lettuce-lined bowls. Cover with plastic wrap and chill until ready to serve.

Norman Weinstein

S ince the Chinese traditionally do not raise cattle for human consumption, the number of beef dishes in the Chinese repertoire is relatively small, and veal dishes are virtually nonexistent. But Norman Weinstein, a teacher of Chinese cooking, has devised three menus that show the adaptability of Chinese techniques to Western ingredients. In the majority of Chinese dishes, foods are cut into bite-size pieces and cooked rapidly in a small amount of oil over very high heat. This classic technique, called "stir frying," is fast and energy-efficient, and allows foods to retain basic nutrients, colors, and flavors. Deep frying and steaming are two other widely used Chinese cooking methods.

The veal and chestnut main course in the first menu combines two cooking methods. Norman Weinstein first deep fries veal cubes to give them a crisp texture and then simmers them slowly in a rich broth seasoned with soy sauce and sugar. The technique, which is close to the Western method of braising, is called "red cooking" and is common in eastern China, around Shanghai. This recipe is the cook's adaptation of a popular Shanghai chicken dish.

The beef with shredded vegetables of Menu 2 is a modified version of a Northern-style dish. Prepared like many of the dishes of that region, it is tossed and glazed with *hoisin* sauce, a sweet Chinese condiment made from soy beans, sugar, vinegar, chilies, and other spices.

Szechwan cuisine is from the western region of China. It is characterized both by fiery chili-flavored sauces and by beef dishes such as shredded beef and tangerine peel, of which the lemon-flavored steak in Menu 3 is a variation.

The balancing of opposites is important in Chinese cuisine; serving this meal on a white plate set on a larger, dark service plate dramatizes the contrasts of color and texture in these recipes. You can achieve the same effect with white plates on shiny black mats of wood, lacquer, or plastic.

Veal with Chestnuts
Ivory and Jade
Brown Rice with Pine Nuts and Raisins

For the main dish, the cook suggests using veal shoulder, which is more economical than loin or leg cuts and holds up well in moist cooking.

Dried chestnuts are available in most Chinese and Italian markets, but the cook prefers the Chinese variety for their slightly smoky taste.

Two types of soy sauce, light and dark, are called for here and in recipes for the following two menus. The dark is slightly darker and thicker than the light; it contains molasses and tastes saltier and sweeter than the light soy.

Most supermarkets now also stock fresh bean curd, or tofu, the soft, white, protein-rich cakes made from soybeans. For the Ivory and Jade recipe, use a firm variety; more fragile types will lose their texture.

WHAT TO DRINK

The ideal accompaniment to the medley of Oriental flavors would be well-chilled beer or ale, but you could also serve a German white wine, such as a *Kabinett*-class Riesling.

SHOPPING LIST AND STAPLES

1½ pounds lean boneless veal shoulder, cut into 1½-inch cubes
4 squares fresh bean curd, preferably firm variety (about 1 pound total weight)
1 pound fresh spinach
4 medium-size carrots (about 1 pound total weight)
4 scallions
2-inch piece fresh ginger
4 or 5 cloves garlic
2¾ cups chicken stock, preferably homemade (see page 13), or canned, plus 2½ cups (optional)
2 cups plus 3 tablespoons peanut oil or corn oil
2 tablespoons Oriental sesame oil
2 tablespoons light soy sauce
2 tablespoons dark soy sauce
1 cup brown rice
4 tablespoons cornstarch
4 ounces dried chestnuts
2 ounces pine nuts
½ cup dark raisins
Two 1½-inch lumps rock sugar, or 3 tablespoons light brown sugar
Salt and freshly ground black pepper
8 tablespoons dry sherry

UTENSILS

14-inch flat-bottom wok with cover
  or large cast-iron Dutch oven with cover
Large cast-iron Dutch oven
  or large heavy-gauge sauté pan
Medium-size heavy-gauge enamel-lined pot with cover
  (if using dried chestnuts)
2 medium-size heavy-gauge saucepans with covers
2 platters
Colander
Salad spinner (optional)
Large mixing bowl plus additional large bowl (optional)
2 small bowls
Cup
Measuring cups and spoons
Chef's knife or slicing cleaver
Paring knife
Chinese metal wok spatulas or 2 wooden spoons
Slotted metal spoon
Deep-fat thermometer (optional)
Vegetable peeler (optional)
Toothpicks

START-TO-FINISH STEPS

The night before: For veal and chestnuts receipe, bring 2 quarts water to a boil in heavy-gauge enamel-lined pot. Add dried chestnuts. Remove from heat, cover, and let stand overnight at room temperature.

1. Follow rice recipe step 1 and Ivory and Jade recipe step 1.
2. While bean curd is soaking and rice is cooking, follow veal recipe steps 1 through 3 and Ivory and Jade recipe step 2.
3. Follow veal recipe steps 4 through 6.
4. Follow Ivory and Jade recipe steps 3 through 5.
5. Follow rice recipe step 2.
6. While rice is cooking, follow veal recipe step 7.
7. While carrots are cooking, follow Ivory and Jade recipe steps 6 through 8.
8. Follow rice recipe step 3.
9. Follow Ivory and Jade recipe steps 9 and 10, and veal recipe step 8.
10. Follow Ivory and Jade recipe step 11, veal recipe step 9, and serve with rice.

Veal with Chestnuts

4 medium-size carrots (about 1 pound total weight)
2 tablespoons light soy sauce
2 tablespoons dark soy sauce
6 tablespoons dry sherry
Two 1½-inch lumps rock sugar, or 3 tablespoons light
   brown sugar
2 scallions
2 cups peanut or corn oil
Thin slice fresh ginger
1½ pounds boneless lean veal shoulder, cut into 1½-inch
   cubes
1 cup dried chestnuts, soaked overnight
1½ cups plus 5 tablespoons chicken stock
3 tablespoons cornstarch

1. Peel carrots and cut into 1½-inch pieces.
2. In small bowl, combine light and dark soy sauces and
sherry. If using brown sugar, add it to soy-sherry mixture
and stir to dissolve.
3. Cut off green part of scallions, reserving bulbs for
another use. Wash, dry, and mince scallion greens.
4. Heat wok or Dutch oven over medium-high heat until it
begins to smoke. Add oil and heat 2 minutes. Add ginger
to pan. If it surfaces immediately, oil is ready (375 degrees
on deep-fat thermometer). Remove ginger and discard.
Add one third of the veal and deep fry, turning frequently
with Chinese metal spatula, until cubes are browned,
about 4 to 5 minutes. Transfer to paper-towel-lined platter. Repeat process for remaining 2 batches.
5. In colander, drain chestnuts and pat dry with paper
towels. Using toothpick, remove any shell matter from
crevices in chestnuts.
6. Pour off all but a film of oil from pan. Add soy-sherry
mixture and bring to a boil. Add veal and stir to coat with
sauce. Add 1½ cups chicken stock and bring to a boil.
Reduce to a simmer, add rock sugar, if using, and dried
chestnuts. Stir, cover, and simmer 10 minutes.
7. Add carrots and recover pan. Cook 20 minutes.
8. With slotted spoon, transfer veal, chestnuts, and carrots to serving bowl. In small bowl, combine cornstarch
with remaining 5 tablespoons stock. Slowly add mixture
to the simmering broth, stirring constantly. When sauce
has reached desired consistency, stop adding mixture.
9. Pour sauce over veal mixture, and garnish with reserved minced scallion greens.

Ivory and Jade

4 squares fresh bean curd, preferably firm variety
   (about 1 pound total weight)
1 pound fresh spinach
2-inch piece fresh ginger
4 or 5 cloves garlic
2 scallions
¾ cup plus 3 tablespoons chicken stock

2 tablespoons dry sherry
3 tablespoons peanut or corn oil
½ teaspoon salt
1 heaping tablespoon cornstarch
Freshly ground black pepper
2 tablespoons Oriental sesame oil

1. In medium-size saucepan, bring 6 cups water to a boil.
Add bean curd and boil 10 minutes. With slotted spoon,
transfer bean curd to large bowl of ice water and let stand
20 minutes.
2. Fill kitchen sink or large bowl with cold water. Rinse
spinach thoroughly. Remove and discard hard stems. Dry
in salad spinner or pat dry with paper towels.
3. Peel ginger and cut crosswise into 10 or 12 slices. Tap
garlic cloves lightly with flat blade of knife or cleaver to
remove skins. Wash and trim scallions. With chef's knife or
cleaver, cut into 1½-inch pieces.
4. In saucepan used for bean curd, combine ¾ cup stock,
ginger, garlic, scallions, and sherry. Bring to a boil, cover,
and simmer 10 minutes.
5. Cut each bean curd square in half, through widest part,
then cut each half into 4 triangles.
6. With slotted spoon, remove ginger, garlic, and scallions
from stock and discard. Transfer stock to Dutch oven or
sauté pan and bring to a boil. Add bean curd and cook 3
minutes. With slotted spoon, transfer bean curd to large
paper-towel-lined platter. Pour stock into small bowl and
reserve.
7. Wipe pan dry. Return pan to stove and heat over medium-high heat until it starts to smoke. Add oil and heat 30
seconds.
8. Add spinach first and then add salt. With metal wok
spatula, stir and press spinach until it is coated with oil
and begins to wilt. Divide among 4 individual plates.
9. In cup, combine cornstarch with remaining 3 tablespoons stock.
10. Return reserved stock to pan, and bring to a boil.
Lower heat to a simmer and slowly add cornstarch mixture, stirring constantly. When sauce has reached desired
consistency, stop adding cornstarch mixture. Return bean
curd to pan and simmer just until heated through.
11. Spoon bean curd and sauce over spinach, sprinkle with
pepper to taste, and drizzle with sesame oil.

Brown Rice with Pine Nuts and Raisins

2½ cups chicken stock or water
1 cup brown rice
½ cup pine nuts (about 2 ounces)
½ cup dark raisins

1. In medium-size saucepan, bring stock or water to a boil.
Add rice, stir once, reduce heat to low, cover, and simmer
35 minutes.
2. Remove cover and add pine nuts and raisins. Stir gently
to mix, replace cover, and cook another 10 minutes.
3. Turn off heat and let rice stand, covered, until ready to
serve.

Celestial Egg Flower Soup
Beef with Shredded Vegetables
White Rice, Chinese Style

The confetti effect of the soup complements the colorful beef with vegetables and the bowls of rice.

The very distinct grain of flank steak makes it easy to shred and ideal for the beef main course of this menu. Soaking the meat in egg whites and cornstarch is a common Chinese cooking technique used to preserve the juices during searing.

Leeks tend to be gritty, so be sure to rinse them thoroughly. The base for the Celestial Egg Flower Soup should be light and delicate so that it does not obscure the flavors of the other ingredients.

You will have egg yolks left over from the beef recipe and, if you choose to use eggs , from the soup recipe; save them for use in a custard dessert.

WHAT TO DRINK

Beer or ale, especially dark beer, is the first choice for this Chinese-style meal. A young and fruity Zinfandel is a good wine selection.

SHOPPING LIST AND STAPLES

1¼ pounds beef flank steak (trimmed weight)
¼ pound small shrimps
Large carrot
Small zucchini

2 medium-size green bell peppers
6 cherry tomatoes
3 leeks (each 1 inch in diameter)
2 large or 4 small scallions
4-inch piece fresh ginger
1 egg plus additional 3 eggs (optional)
10-ounce package frozen peas
6 cups chicken stock, preferably homemade
    (see page 13), or canned
7 to 9 tablespoons peanut or corn oil
1 tablespoon Oriental sesame oil (optional)
1 tablespoon dark soy sauce
1 tablespoon light soy sauce
½ cup *hoisin* sauce
6 dried Chinese black mushrooms (about 2 ounces total
    weight), or ½ pound fresh mushrooms
2 cups long-grain rice
¼ cup plus 1 tablespoon cornstarch
Pinch of sugar
3 tablespoons dry sherry plus additional sherry
    (if using canned broth)

UTENSILS

14-inch flat-bottom wok or 10- to 12-inch Dutch oven or
    heavy-gauge sauté pan
2 medium-size heavy-gauge saucepans, one with cover
2 platters
Medium-size bowl
5 small bowls
Measuring cups and spoons
Chef's knife or slicing cleaver
Paring knife
Chinese metal wok spatulas or 2 wooden spoons
Large slotted spoon
Wooden spoon
Whisk
Soup ladle
Vegetable peeler

START-TO-FINISH STEPS

1. Follow rice recipe steps 1 and 2.
2. Follow soup recipe steps 1 through 6.
3. Follow beef recipe steps 1 and 2.
4. While beef is in egg-white mixture, follow rice recipe

steps 3 and 4, and beef recipe steps 3 through 7.
5. Follow soup recipe steps 7 through 15 and serve.
6. Follow rice recipe step 5.
7. Follow beef recipe steps 8 through 10 and serve with rice.

RECIPES

Celestial Egg Flower Soup

6 dried Chinese black mushrooms (about 2 ounces total
    weight), or ½ pound fresh mushrooms
2 large or 4 small scallions
6 cups chicken stock
4 to 5 thin slices fresh ginger
Pinch of sugar
Dry sherry (if using canned stock)
¼ pound small shrimps
Small zucchini
1 leek (about 1 inch in diameter)
6 cherry tomatoes
¼ cup cornstarch
3 eggs (optional)
½ cup frozen peas
1 tablespoon Oriental sesame oil (optional)

1. If using dried mushrooms, place mushrooms in small bowl. Cover with boiling water and let soak 15 to 20 minutes, or until softened.
2. Wash scallions, trim off ends, and cut in half. In medium-size saucepan, bring chicken stock, ginger, scallions, and a pinch of sugar to a simmer. If using canned broth, add ⅔ can cold water and sherry to taste. Simmer 5 minutes. Using slotted spoon, remove scallions and ginger, and discard. Remove pan from heat and set aside.
3. Peel and devein shrimp. Rinse under cold water. Set aside.
4. Wash zucchini and cut enough into ⅜-inch dice to measure ½ cup.
5. Cut green portion from leek, reserving white for another use. Trim off tops of greens and discard. Slit remaining green portion lengthwise into 6 to 8 strips. Rinse thoroughly in cold water to remove any grit. With chef's knife or slicing cleaver, cut crosswise to yield ¼ cup.
6. Cut each tomato in half.
7. Drain mushrooms and discard tough stems. Cut mushrooms into quarters. If using fresh mushrooms, clean with damp paper towels and proceed as for dried.

8. In small bowl, mix cornstarch with ¾ cup stock.
9. If using eggs, separate them into 2 small bowls and reserve yolks for another use. With whisk, beat egg whites until frothy.
10. Return stock to a simmer. Add mushrooms and leeks, and simmer 2 minutes. Add zucchini and simmer 30 seconds.
11. Bring soup to a simmer. Stir cornstarch mixture to recombine. Stirring constantly, slowly add cornstarch mixture to the soup. When soup has reached desired consistency, stop adding cornstarch mixture.
12. Add tomatoes and shrimp to soup. Stir 30 seconds.
13. Reduce heat to low. Slowly pour egg white into thickened soup. Allow to set 10 seconds, then agitate soup slowly with a ladle to bring egg white to top.
14. Add peas to soup, stirring to break up frozen block.
15. Transfer soup to a tureen. Top with sesame oil, if desired, and serve.

Beef with Shredded Vegetables

1¼ pounds beef flank steak (trimmed weight)
1 tablespoon light soy sauce
3 tablespoons dry sherry
1 egg
1 tablespoon cornstarch
3-inch piece fresh ginger
Large carrot
2 medium-size green bell peppers
2 leeks (each about 1 inch in diameter)
½ cup *hoisin* sauce
1 tablespoon dark soy sauce
7 to 9 tablespoons peanut or corn oil

1. Lay steak on cutting surface. Holding sharp chef's knife or slicing cleaver at a very low angle, cut steak across grain into 3-inch slices. Then, cutting with, not against, the grain, shred the slices. (See diagrams below.)
2. Place shreds in medium-size bowl. Add light soy sauce and 2 tablespoons sherry, and toss. Separate egg, reserving yolk for another use. Add egg white to meat-sherry mixture and toss to coat shreds evenly. Dust surface with cornstarch and toss again. Let stand at least 15 minutes.
3. Peel ginger. Cut lengthwise into 8 thin slices. Make stacks of 3 to 4 slices each and cut into thin 3-inch shreds.

4. Peel carrot and cut into 3-inch sections. Cut a thin lengthwise slice from each section so it will lie flat. Place on cutting surface and, with chef's knife or slicing cleaver, cut each section into thin slices, then into shreds.
5. Core, seed, and derib peppers. Cut into 3-inch shreds.
6. Cut green portion from leeks. Reserve whites for another use. Trim off tops of greens and discard.
7. In small bowl, combine *hoisin* sauce, remaining tablespoon dry sherry, and dark soy sauce.
8. Heat wok, Dutch oven, or heavy-gauge sauté pan over high heat until it smokes. Add 5 tablespoons oil. Heat until a shred of ginger sizzles on contact. Remove ginger and discard. Add one third of the beef shreds. Using metal wok spatulas or 2 wooden spoons, stir fry beef until lightly browned, about 2 to 3 minutes. With slotted spoon, transfer beef to paper-towel-lined platter. Repeat process with remaining 2 batches.
9. Add 2 more tablespoons oil to pan if needed—do *not* use unless absolutely necessary—and heat 10 seconds. Add ginger shreds and carrots, and stir fry until carrots are slightly wilted, about 2 to 3 minutes. Add peppers and stir fry 15 seconds. Add leeks and stir fry another 15 seconds.
10. Transfer vegetables to another paper-towel-lined platter. Add 2 more tablespoons oil to pan and heat 15 seconds. Add *hoisin* mixture and stir until bubbly. Add beef and vegetables, and stir to mix well. When heated through, transfer to serving platter.

White Rice, Chinese Style

1. Place 2 cups long-grain rice in medium-size heavy-gauge saucepan. Add enough cold water to cover rice by 1 inch and bring to a boil over medium-high heat. Cover pan and reduce heat to very low.
2. Simmer rice 25 minutes.
3. Lift cover of saucepan and fork up a few grains of rice. Quickly replace cover. Rice is done when center of grain is still slightly firm.
4. Off heat, let rice stand, covered, for at least 15 minutes to absorb any liquid and steam still in pan. Rice will fluff up. (*Note:* If saucepan has sides thick enough to retain heat, rice can stand for as long as 30 minutes.)
5. When ready to serve, lift cover and fluff rice with fork. Turn into individual serving bowls.

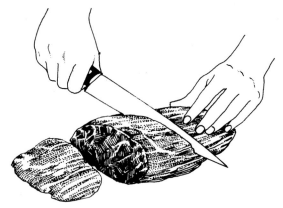

1. Cut steak across grain into 3-inch slices.

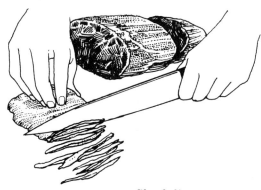

2. Shred slices, cutting with grain.

Lemon-Flavored Steak
Braised Black Mushrooms with Snow Peas
Peppered Noodles

The spicy noodles, which get their bite from serrano chilies, stand up to the tangy beef dish, flavored with lemon peel.

Shell steak (sometimes sold as strip steak or beef top loin steak) is used for this menu's main course. Both the ginger and the lemon peel in this dish are meant to be eaten, so slice the ginger very thin. Some of the white pith of the lemon should be included with the peel to add texture and bitterness.

Fragrant, meaty black Chinese mushrooms contrast dramatically with the crisp, fresh snow peas, and there really is no substitute for them in this vegetable dish. Dried Chinese mushrooms are available in Chinese markets and in many specialty food shops. If you cannot find fresh snow peas, substitute frozen ones. Thaw them before using.

The oyster sauce called for in this dish is a rich Cantonese condiment made from powdered fermented oysters and soy sauce. You can buy it in the Oriental-foods section of most supermarkets.

WHAT TO DRINK

These hot-and-sour flavors go well with an Alsatian or California Gewürztraminer, which are dry and spicy.

SHOPPING LIST AND STAPLES

2 boneless shell steaks, 1 inch thick, trimmed of fat, and
    tails removed (each about 1 pound)
½ pound snow peas
6 to 8 fresh serrano chilies, or fresh or canned jalapeño
    peppers
Large red bell pepper
Large bunch scallions
1 lemon
1½-inch piece fresh ginger
¾ cup chicken stock, preferably homemade (see page 13),
    or canned
3 cups plus 1 tablespoon peanut or corn oil
¼ cup Oriental sesame oil
3 tablespoons light soy sauce
2 tablespoons oyster sauce
3 tablespoons Worcestershire sauce
20 dried Chinese black mushrooms, of uniform size, or 1
    pound fresh mushrooms
¾ pound vermicelli
¼ cup cornstarch
2 tablespoons sugar
2 tablespoons coarse salt
Freshly ground black pepper
3 tablespoons dry sherry
3 tablespoons Cognac or brandy

UTENSILS

Large stockpot or kettle with cover
14-inch flat-bottomed wok or large Dutch oven or heavy-
    gauge sauté pan
Medium-size skillet with cover

Medium-size saucepan
Small enamel-lined saucepan
2 large mixing bowls
4 small mixing bowls
Large platter
Colander
Measuring cups and spoons
Chef's knife or slicing cleaver
Paring knife
Chinese metal wok spatulas or 2 wooden spoons
Slotted metal spoon
Small sharp scissors
Deep-fat thermometer
Rubber gloves

START-TO-FINISH STEPS

1. Follow mushrooms recipe step 1. While water is coming to a boil, follow steak recipe steps 1 and 2.
2. Follow mushrooms recipe step 2.
3. While mushrooms are soaking, follow steak recipe steps 3 through 6 and pasta recipe steps 1 through 4.
4. Follow mushrooms recipe steps 3 through 7.
5. While mushrooms cook, follow pasta recipe steps 5 and 6.
6. About 5 minutes before mushrooms are done, follow steak recipe step 7.
7. Follow pasta recipe step 7 and steak recipe steps 8 through 13.
8. Follow mushrooms recipe steps 8 and 9, pasta recipe steps 8 and 9, and serve with steak.

RECIPES

Lemon-Flavored Steak

2 boneless shell steaks, 1 inch thick, trimmed of fat, and
    tails removed (each about 1 pound)
¼ cup cornstarch
1 lemon
Large red bell pepper
4 scallions
1½-inch piece fresh ginger
1 tablespoon light soy sauce
3 tablespoons Cognac or brandy
2 cups peanut or corn oil
1 tablespoon sugar

1. With very sharp chef's knife, cut shell steaks in half lengthwise. Holding knife at as low an angle as possible to the meat, cut each half into six 1-inch-thick slices. Place in large mixing bowl and sprinkle with 3 tablespoons cornstarch. With your hands, toss slices to coat evenly with cornstarch. Shake off any excess starch. Let steak pieces stand for at least 15 minutes.
2. Cut lemon peel, including pith, into ½-inch strips. Squeeze lemon to measure 2 tablespoons juice. Set aside.
3. Core, seed, and derib pepper. Cut pepper lengthwise into quarters. On the bias, cut each quarter into 6 pieces.

4. Wash scallions and trim off ends. Remove green portions and reserve for another dish. With chef's knife, cut white portions, on the bias, into 1-inch sections.

5. Peel ginger and cut crosswise into ⅛-inch-thick slices.

6. For the sauce, combine remaining tablespoon cornstarch, lemon juice, soy sauce, and Cognac in small bowl.

7. Heat wok, Dutch oven, or sauté pan over high heat until it begins to smoke. Add oil and heat 2 minutes, or until a sliver of ginger rises immediately to the surface (375 degrees on deep-fat thermometer). Remove ginger and discard.

8. Add steak, 6 slices at a time. Deep fry until crusty, about 1 minute. With slotted metal spoon, remove steak, wait 15 seconds, and return to oil for another 10 to 15 seconds. Transfer steak to paper-towel-lined platter. Repeat process for remaining slices.

9. Pour off all but 3 tablespoons oil from pan and heat 10 seconds. Add ginger slices and lemon peel. Stir fry vigorously 1 minute.

10. Add scallions and peppers and stir fry another minute.

11. Return steak slices to pan. Add sugar and toss.

12. With spatula, move contents of pan to one side. Stir sauce mixture to recombine, and then pour it down side of pan into cleared space. Stir sauce with point of spatula until thickened. Incorporate remaining ingredients, stirring until they are evenly coated with sauce.

13. Transfer to serving platter and cover loosely with foil.

Braised Black Mushrooms with Snow Peas

20 dried Chinese black mushrooms, of uniform size, or 1
   pound fresh mushrooms
½ pound snow peas
¾ cup chicken stock
2 tablespoons oyster sauce
3 tablespoons dry sherry
1 tablespoon sugar

1. In medium-size saucepan, bring 3 cups water to a boil.

2. If using dried mushrooms, place them in large bowl. Add the 3 cups boiling water and let soak at least 15 minutes. If using fresh mushrooms, clean with damp paper towels. Remove stems.

3. Remove caps, strings, and bottom tips from snow peas.

4. For sauce, combine remaining ingredients in small bowl.

5. When soaked mushrooms are soft and spongy, drain them and squeeze dry. With small sharp scissors, remove stems and discard.

6. In medium-size saucepan, bring 3 cups water to a boil.

7. In medium-size skillet, bring sauce to a boil over medium-high heat. Add mushrooms, and stir to coat with sauce. If using dried mushrooms, cover skillet and simmer 25 minutes; if using fresh, cover and simmer 10 minutes.

8. Place colander in sink. Add snow peas to the boiling water and stir. As soon as they turn bright green (no longer than 10 seconds), pour peas and water into colander. Rinse peas under cold running water. Shake colander a few times to drain. Pat peas dry with paper towels.

9. Remove skillet cover and add snow peas. Stir gently 10 to 15 seconds, just until peas are coated with sauce. Transfer to platter and serve immediately.

Peppered Noodles

4 scallions
6 to 8 fresh serrano chilies, or fresh or canned jalapeño
   peppers
1 cup plus 1 tablespoon peanut or corn oil
¼ cup Oriental sesame oil
2 tablespoons light soy sauce
3 tablespoons Worcestershire sauce
2 tablespoons coarse salt
¾ pound vermicelli
Freshly ground black pepper

1. Wash scallions and trim off ends. Mince green portions and reserve whites for another purpose.

2. Wearing thin rubber gloves, cut off and discard tops of chilies. With paring knife, split chilies lengthwise and, using tip of knife, remove seeds and membranes. Rinse under cold water and pat dry with paper towels. With chef's knife, cut chilies lengthwise into thin strips.

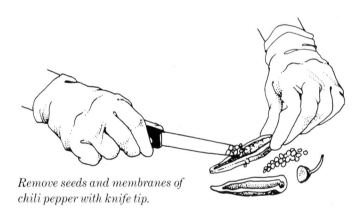

Remove seeds and membranes of chili pepper with knife tip.

3. In small bowl, combine peanut and sesame oils.

4. In small enamel-lined saucepan, heat 3 tablespoons of the oil mixture over medium-high heat. Add chili shreds and cook, stirring, 20 seconds. Remove pan from heat and reserve.

5. In large stockpot or kettle, bring 5 quarts water to a boil over high heat.

6. In small bowl, combine soy and Worcestershire sauces.

7. Add salt and 1 tablespoon oil mixture to the boiling water. Still over high heat, add vermicelli, one third at a time, waiting for water to return to a boil before adding each remaining third. Cook until *al dente*, about 5 minutes, testing frequently. In colander, drain and then rinse vermicelli under cold water. Shake colander a few times to drain thoroughly. Return pasta to pot and top with ¼ cup of the oil mixture. Toss until well coated, and cover.

8. For sauce, add chilies and soy sauce-Worcestershire mixture to remaining oil and stir to combine.

9. Add sauce to pasta. Top with minced scallions and freshly ground pepper to taste. Toss and serve immediately.

Victoria Fahey

Before Victoria Fahey became a professional cook, she studied art. Now, as she works with foods, she uses their colors, textures, smells, and tastes to produce meals of great appeal to all the senses. As a seacoast resident, she gathers her own shellfish, and she is also able to pick wild mushrooms from nearby woods. In addition, she has access to the fine restaurants, well-stocked grocery stores, and exotic specialty food shops in San Francisco. Thus, her menus exhibit both cosmopolitan and country touches.

A well-composed meal, Menu 1 is representative of how Victoria Fahey blends tastes and contrasts textures and colors. The avocado soup appears smooth, yet conceals diced avocado, tomato, and chives. The subtle flavor of the soup is counterbalanced by the highly spiced main-course beef salad.

For Menu 2, the cook presents an all-American entrée of oven-roasted beef back ribs basted with a spicy barbecue sauce and served with oven-roasted potatoes. To offset the basic quality of the meat and potatoes, she serves foil-baked gingered carrots and a Romaine salad with walnuts, walnut oil, and Roquefort cheese.

Menu 3 is a company meal of Italian-style peppery veal chops, served with sautéed red-pepper strips and pancetta (Italian bacon), and fresh pasta tossed with toasted pine nuts and Parmesan cheese on the side.

Serve the marinated beef salad on a bed of shredded lettuce with lime slices, sesame seeds, crushed red pepper, and a border of melon slices. Garnish the chilled avocado soup with whole chive stalks arranged in a pattern. Dessert is unhulled whole strawberries and dried apricots dipped in white and dark chocolate.

57

Chilled Avocado Soup
Marinated Beef Salad
Fruit Dipped in White and Dark Chocolate

The exotic chilled beef salad, the entrée for this summer meal, features flavorings often associated with Southeast Asian cuisines: lime juice, fresh ginger, coriander, mint leaves, sesame oil, and the optional red pepper flakes and sesame seeds. You can make the salad with thinly sliced rare roast beef from a delicatessen. Or, you can use leftover rare roast beef that was cooked at home. If you like raw beef, a high-quality sirloin steak (sometimes sold as beef loin sirloin steak) sliced very thin and used raw is another alternative.

In this light menu, the dessert is sweet as well as refreshing. Coating fruit with melted chocolate, as you do here, is a variation on a classic candy-making technique. Use semisweet or bittersweet chocolate, as you prefer. Real chocolate, used for most candy or baking, is made from chocolate liquor—part cocoa butter and part cocoa solids. Read labels carefully and avoid imitation chocolate products. White chocolate, which this recipe also calls for, is technically not a chocolate at all because it does not contain any chocolate liquor. Made with cocoa butter, sugar, vanillin, and other flavorings, white chocolate tastes like mellow milk chocolate. Victoria Fahey believes the best chocolate is from Belgium. It is generally available in specialty food stores, but if you have difficulty finding it buy baking chocolate from your supermarket, or use top-quality pure chocolate candy bars. Melt the chocolate slowly in the top of a double boiler to keep it from scorching, and keep it free from moisture; otherwise it becomes granular. Chop the chocolate into small pieces first to make the melting easier. And chill the fruit before you dip it, so that the chocolate will harden on it faster.

WHAT TO DRINK

You need a crisp, dry white wine with good body and flavor: a California or an Italian Sauvignon Blanc, or a good-quality French Sancerre.

SHOPPING LIST AND STAPLES

1½ pounds cooked rare roast beef or raw sirloin
Large head Romaine lettuce
3 medium-size avocados, preferably dark, knobby Haas variety (about 1½ pounds total weight)
Medium-size tomato
4 limes

1 lemon (if not using lime juice for soup)
2 small cantaloupes (½ to ¾ pound each)
1 pint strawberries
Small bunch fresh cilantro or parsley
Small bunch fresh mint, or 1 teaspoon dried
1 bunch fresh chives
1-inch piece fresh ginger
½ pint heavy cream
2 cups chicken stock, preferably homemade (see page 13), or canned
6 tablespoons peanut oil
1 teaspoon sesame oil
1 tablespoon Dijon mustard
4 ounces dark chocolate
2 ounces white chocolate
½ pound dried apricots or other fresh or dried fruit
1 tablespoon sesame seeds (optional)
Red pepper flakes (optional)
1½ teaspoons salt

UTENSILS

Food processor or blender
Electric mixer
Large heavy-gauge skillet or sauté pan
Small heavy-gauge skillet (optional)
2 double boilers or 2 heatproof mixing bowls to fit in separate saucepans
2 medium-size mixing bowls
Small bowl
Serving platter
Large flat plate or platter
Salad spinner (optional)
Measuring cups and spoons
Chef's knife
Paring knife
Slotted metal spatula
Rubber spatula
2 wooden spoons
Juicer (optional)
Grater

START-TO-FINISH STEPS

One hour and 15 minutes ahead: Follow fruit recipe step 1.

1. Follow fruit recipe step 2.

2. In small heavy-gauge skillet, toast sesame seeds for beef recipe, if using, over medium-high heat, until they smell toasty and turn a light brown. Shake skillet frequently to keep seeds from scorching.
3. Follow soup recipe steps 1 through 3.
4. Follow beef recipe steps 1 through 5.
5. Follow soup recipe step 4 and serve.
6. Follow beef recipe steps 6 and 7 and serve.
7. Serve chocolate-dipped fruits for dessert.

RECIPES

Chilled Avocado Soup

3 medium-size avocados, preferably dark, knobby Haas variety
1 lime or lemon
2 cups chicken stock
1 cup heavy cream
1 tablespoon Dijon mustard
1 teaspoon salt
Medium-size tomato
1 bunch fresh chives

1. Put soup bowls, medium-size mixing bowl, and beaters in freezer to chill.
2. Peel and pit avocados. Juice lime or lemon. In food processor or blender, purée 2 avocados, chicken stock, ½ cup cream, mustard, 1 to 2 tablespoons lime or lemon juice, and salt until very smooth.
3. Halve and seed tomato. Cut tomato and remaining avocado into ¼-inch dice. Mince enough chives to measure 1 tablespoon, reserving unchopped stalks for garnish. Remove soup bowls from freezer. Spoon a portion of avocado chunks, tomato, and minced chives into each bowl. Top with puréed soup. Cover with plastic wrap and refrigerate until ready to serve.
4. Just before serving, whip remaining ½ cup cream in chilled bowl, with chilled beaters. Garnish soup with whipped cream and whole chive stalks, decoratively arranged.

Marinated Beef Salad

Large head Romaine lettuce
3 limes
1-inch piece fresh ginger
Small bunch fresh cilantro or parsley
Small bunch fresh mint, or 1 teaspoon dried
6 tablespoons peanut oil
1 teaspoon sesame oil
½ teaspoon salt
1½ pounds cooked rare roast beef or raw sirloin
2 small cantaloupes (½ to ¾ pound each)
1 tablespoon sesame seeds (optional)
Red pepper flakes (optional)

1. Put serving platter in freezer to chill. Wash lettuce and dry in salad spinner or pat dry with paper towels.

2. Grate lime rind. Squeeze enough lime juice to measure 4 tablespoons, reserving any extra. Cut 1 lime into wedges for garnish. Peel and mince ginger. Wash, dry, and chop cilantro and mint, if using fresh, to measure 1½ tablespoons each. Reserve unchopped cilantro and fresh mint for garnish. For dressing, combine 4 tablespoons peanut oil, sesame oil, salt, ginger root, chopped cilantro, and mint in small bowl. Set aside.
3. With chef's knife, slice meat into strips ⅛ to ¼ inch wide, and 1 to 1½ inches long, if not already sliced.
4. To cook raw meat, unless you prefer to serve it raw, heat remaining 2 tablespoons peanut oil in large heavy-gauge skillet or sauté pan over high heat. Add meat and cook, stirring constantly, just until meat is no longer pink, 30 to 60 seconds.
5. Using slotted metal spatula, transfer meat to chilled platter. Arrange cooked sirloin, precooked roast beef, or raw sirloin in single layer. Pour dressing over meat, cover loosely, and refrigerate until chilled.
6. Transfer meat and dressing to medium-size bowl and clean platter. Peel, seed, and slice cantaloupe and arrange around edge of platter. Shred lettuce and form bed in center. Using wooden spoons, toss meat with dressing to coat well. Spoon meat over lettuce. Sprinkle with reserved lime juice to taste.
7. Just before serving, garnish with mint, cilantro, and lime wedges. Top with sesame seeds and sprinkle lightly with red pepper flakes, if desired. Serve additional red pepper flakes on the side.

Fruit Dipped in White and Dark Chocolate

1 pint strawberries, unhulled, or 2 Navel oranges
½ pound dried apricots, or other fresh or dried fruit
4 ounces dark chocolate
2 ounces white chocolate

1. Rinse strawberries briefly in cold water. Gently pat dry with paper towels and let stand for at least 1 hour, turning once, to make sure all moisture has evaporated. If using oranges, peel and remove as much white pith as possible. Section with sharp paring knife by cutting between membranes. Arrange on paper towels and proceed as for strawberries. Refrigerate fruit until ready to use.
2. In 2 double boilers, one for dark chocolate and one for white, or in 2 bowls set in separate saucepans, melt chocolate over—not in—simmering water. Line large flat plate or platter with wax paper. When chocolate is melted, hold a strawberry by its hull and dip about two thirds of berry in chocolate, leaving some red showing. Lightly scrape one side of strawberry on edge of double boiler or bowl to prevent a puddle of chocolate from forming on wax paper. Set strawberry on wax paper, scraped side down. Repeat for remaining berries. Dip some of the strawberries in white and some in dark chocolate. If you like, dip berry first in one and, when that hardens, dip partially in the other. Or, with a teaspoon, drizzle chocolate of one color over the other. Repeat dipping process with fruits of your choice.

Hearts of Romaine with Walnuts, Roquefort, and Oranges
Oven-Barbecued Beef Back Ribs
Gingered Carrots in Foil / Roast Potatoes

Victoria Fahey provides an indoors alternative to barbecuing by oven-roasting beef back ribs in a barbecue sauce. More flavorful and less fatty than short ribs, these back ribs are roasted quickly at a high temperature so that they are crisp on the outside and slightly rare on the inside. The spicy sauce adds flavor and prevents the meat from drying out.

Wrapping food before cooking tenderizes it and protects it from burning. Foil-wrapped foods, such as the gingered carrots here, steam quickly. Cut the foil package open when you serve the carrots, releasing a burst of appetizing

Beef back ribs, glazed with barbecue sauce, are the focal point of this informal meal. Served family style, the ribs are accompanied by roasted potatoes, ginger-flavored carrots, and hearts of Romaine lettuce.

aroma. Fresh ginger is available in many supermarkets or in Chinese groceries. Select ginger that is hard, smooth-skinned, and tan in color. For information on storing it, see page 15.

Toasted walnuts and walnut oil give the salad a rich, nutty taste. Walnut oil, more expensive than extra-virgin olive oil, is sold in specialty food shops. It turns rancid easily; close it tightly after each use and store it in your refrigerator.

WHAT TO DRINK

The piquant spicing of this menu will taste best with a dry and fruity red wine: a California Zinfandel, a French Beaujolais, or an Italian Dolcetto.

8 to 12 beef back ribs (about 4 to 6 pounds total weight)

1½ pounds boiling potatoes, preferably, or red-skinned or baking potatoes

1½ pounds carrots

3 large or 4 small heads Romaine lettuce (about 2½ pounds total weight)

2 oranges

1 lemon

1-inch piece fresh ginger, or ½ teaspoon ground ginger

4 tablespoons unsalted butter

4 ounces Roquefort cheese

2 tablespoons walnut oil

2 tablespoons cider vinegar

1 cup catsup

4 ounces walnut halves

1 cup plus 1 tablespoon brown sugar

1 teaspoon dry mustard

½ teaspoon ground cumin

⅛ teaspoon celery seed (optional)

Cayenne pepper

Salt

Freshly ground pepper

Small heavy-gauge saucepan

Two 9 x 12-inch shallow baking sheets

9 x 13-inch jelly-roll pan

Rectangular ovenproof baking dish

Large bowl

Medium-size bowl
Small bowl
Salad spinner (optional)
Measuring cups and spoons
Chef's knife
Paring knife
Spatula
Juicer (optional)
Scissors
Basting brush
Vegetable peeler

START-TO-FINISH STEPS

1. Follow potatoes recipe steps 1 through 3.
2. While potatoes are baking, follow carrots recipe steps 1 through 5 and Romaine recipe steps 1 and 2.
3. Follow ribs recipe steps 1 and 2, and carrots recipe step 6.
4. While ribs, carrots, and potatoes are cooking, follow Romaine recipe steps 3 and 4.
5. Follow potatoes recipe step 4.
6. Remove carrots and potatoes from oven, cover potatoes loosely with foil, and set on stove top to keep warm.
7. Follow ribs recipe step 3, Romaine recipe step 5, and then ribs recipe step 4. While ribs are browning, serve Romaine salad.
8. Follow ribs recipe step 5.
9. Just before ribs are done, check carrots and potatoes to see if they are hot enough. If necessary, return to oven briefly.
10. Follow ribs recipe step 6 and serve with potatoes and carrots.

RECIPES

Hearts of Romaine with Walnuts, Roquefort, and Oranges

½ cup walnut halves
2 oranges
3 large or 4 small heads Romaine lettuce
1 lemon
2 tablespoons walnut oil
Pinch of Cayenne pepper
Salt
4 ounces Roquefort cheese

1. Break walnut halves into smaller pieces. Arrange in single layer on baking sheet and toast in 375-degree oven 3 to 5 minutes.
2. While walnuts are toasting, cut several strips of orange rind. Cut lengthwise into julienne strips and then crosswise into ⅛-inch dice. Measure 1 tablespoon and set aside.
3. Remove tough outer leaves from Romaine and reserve for another use. Separate tender inner leaves. Wash, if necessary, and dry in salad spinner or pat dry with paper towels. Arrange on round platter, radiating out from center, with larger leaves on bottom, smaller on top. Cover and refrigerate.
4. Halve oranges and squeeze enough juice to measure ½ cup. Squeeze lemon to measure 1 to 2 tablespoons juice. In small bowl, combine orange juice, lemon juice, walnut oil, Cayenne, and salt to taste. Set aside until ready to serve.
5. Crumble Roquefort. Stir dressing to recombine and drizzle over greens. Sprinkle with walnuts, crumbled Roquefort, and reserved orange rind and serve.

Oven-Barbecued Beef Back Ribs

1 cup catsup
1 cup brown sugar
2 tablespoons cider vinegar
1 teaspoon dry mustard
½ teaspoon ground cumin
⅛ teaspoon celery seed (optional)
Cayenne pepper
Salt
Freshly ground pepper
8 to 12 beef back ribs
   (about 4 to 6 pounds total weight)

1. For barbecue sauce, combine catsup, sugar, vinegar, dry mustard, cumin, celery seed, if using, and Cayenne pepper to taste in medium-size bowl.
2. Line baking sheet with foil. Salt and pepper ribs, and arrange in single layer on foil-lined sheet. Bake 30 minutes at 375 degrees.
3. Remove ribs from oven and raise oven temperature to 450 degrees.
4. Stir barbecue sauce to recombine and brush ribs generously with it. Return ribs to oven for 10 minutes.
5. Brush ribs with sauce a second time and return to oven for another 5 to 10 minutes.
6. When ribs look shiny and crispy, remove from oven.

Gingered Carrots in Foil

1½ pounds carrots
1-inch piece fresh ginger, or ½ teaspoon ground ginger
1 tablespoon brown sugar
Salt
1 tablespoon unsalted butter

1. Peel carrots and cut on diagonal into ⅛- to ¼-inch-thick slices.
2. If using fresh ginger, peel and finely grate enough to measure 1 teaspoon.
3. In large bowl, combine carrots, ginger, brown sugar, and salt to taste, and toss to coat carrots evenly.
4. Cut four 12 x 20-inch sheets of aluminum foil. Butter foil and fold in half. With scissors, round corners.
5. Place a portion of carrots onto one half of each foil sheet and dot with about 1 teaspoon butter. Fold other half of foil over carrots and roll and crimp edges tightly so that no steam can escape.

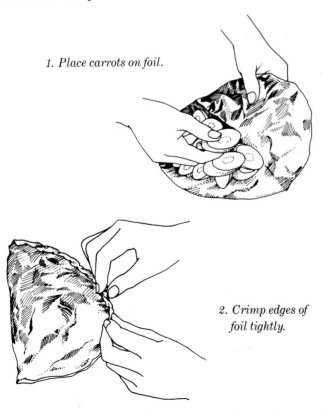

1. Place carrots on foil.

*2. Crimp edges of
foil tightly.*

6. Place packages in ovenproof baking dish and bake 30 minutes in 375-degree oven.

Roast Potatoes

3 tablespoons unsalted butter
1½ pounds boiling potatoes, preferably, or red-skinned or
    baking potatoes
Salt

1. Preheat oven to 375 degrees. In small heavy-gauge saucepan, melt 1 tablespoon butter. Pour into jelly-roll pan, tilting pan to distribute butter evenly.
2. Wash potatoes and cut into 1-inch-thick slices. Do not peel. In jelly-roll pan, arrange slices in single layer. Dot with remaining butter. Pour ¾ cup water into pan. Salt potatoes to taste.
3. Place pan on bottom rack of oven and roast potatoes 30 minutes.
4. After 30 minutes, pour off any remaining water and return potatoes to oven. When bottoms of potatoes have browned, about 10 minutes, turn them over and roast until brown on other side, 10 to 15 minutes.

■■■■■■■■■

ADDED TOUCH

The cutting technique described in step 2 is an efficient way to work with juicy mangoes.

Mangoes with Whipped Cream and Crystallized Ginger

2 mangoes
1 tablespoon crystallized ginger
1 cup heavy cream
1 tablespoon sugar

1. In freezer, chill bowl and beaters for whipping cream.
2. Cut mangoes lengthwise down each side as close to the pit as possible. Gently pull apart and remove pit. With paring knife, being careful not to cut through skin, score mango so it separates into cubes. Now turn mango inside out by pushing on skin side until scored side curves outward. Over mixing bowl, carefully cut off protruding squares of mango, letting mango fall into bowl. Cover and refrigerate.
3. With chef's knife, chop ginger into tiny pieces, about 1/16 inch square.
4. Remove bowl and beaters from freezer and whip cream. Fold in sugar and ginger. Make nests of whipped cream on 4 plates. Spoon mango cubes into center.

Peppered Veal Chops
Sautéed Red Peppers with Pancetta
Pasta with Toasted Pine Nuts and Parmesan Cheese

Arrange this colorful company dinner of peppered veal chops, sautéed red peppers with pancetta, and pasta with pine nuts and Parmesan cheese on plain dinnerware. Garnish the red pepper strips with parsley.

These meaty veal chops are cut from the loin. For a more æsthetic-looking serving and for more even cooking, tie each chop securely with kitchen string: Cut string into 4 foot-long pieces. Tie 1 piece around each chop to make a tuck in the "tail" at the bottom of the T-shaped bone (see diagram on opposite page).

The sautéed red peppers are served with pancetta, an unsmoked Italian bacon cured in salt and spices. Pancetta is usually available in Italian grocery stores.

The salad dressing contains another Italian ingredient, balsamic vinegar. This dense, rich vinegar has a pungent aroma and a mellow sweet-sour taste. It is worth looking for in specialty food shops, though red wine or sherry vinegars are acceptable alternatives.

WHAT TO DRINK

To complement the flavors of this menu, choose a dry, medium-bodied red wine, either a Chianti Classico Riserva or a California Merlot.

SHOPPING LIST AND STAPLES

Four ¾-inch-thick veal loin chops (about ½ to ¾ pound each)
¼ pound pancetta (about 5 slices), or 2 ounces bacon
6 red bell peppers (about 1½ pounds total weight)
Small bunch fresh parsley (optional)
Small bunch fresh oregano, or 1 teaspoon dried
3 large cloves garlic
4 tablespoons unsalted butter
¼ pound Parmesan cheese
2 tablespoons olive oil
2 tablespoons balsamic vinegar
½ pound dry or fresh egg pasta, such as fettuccine
2 ounces pine nuts
Salt and freshly ground black pepper

UTENSILS

Large saucepan or stockpot with cover
Large heavy-gauge skillet or sauté pan with cover
Small heavy-gauge skillet or sauté pan
9 x 12-inch shallow baking sheet
Medium-size bowl
Small bowl or cup
Colander

Measuring cups and spoons
Chef's knife
Paring knife
Slotted spoon
Grater
Mallet or rolling pin (optional)
4 feet cotton string (optional)

START-TO-FINISH STEPS

1. For veal recipe, adjust pepper mill to coarse grind and grind enough pepper to measure 4 teaspoons. Or place peppercorns between 2 sheets of wax paper and crush with mallet or rolling pin. Follow veal chops recipe steps 1 and 2.

2. If using fresh oregano, strip leaves to measure 2 teaspoons. Follow red peppers recipe steps 1 through 4.

3. While peppers are cooking, follow pasta recipe steps 1 through 3 and veal recipe step 3.

4. Follow pasta recipe step 4 and veal recipe step 4.

5. Follow pasta recipe steps 5 and 6, and peppers recipe step 5.

6. Follow veal recipe step 5, pasta recipe step 7, peppers recipe step 6, and serve.

RECIPES

Peppered Veal Chops

Four ¾-inch-thick veal loin chops
4 teaspoons coarsely ground black pepper
Salt

1. Cut string into 4 foot-long pieces. Tie 1 piece around each veal chop to make tuck in "tail" at bottom of T-shaped bone. This step is optional but makes for a neater shape and slightly more even cooking.

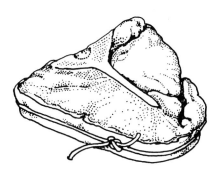

For a neat shape, tie string around each veal chop.

2. Rub approximately ½ teaspoon pepper into both sides of each chop. Sprinkle with salt to taste and set aside at room temperature.

3. Preheat broiler. Place oven rack approximately 4 inches from broiler element.

4. Arrange chops in single layer on shallow baking sheet. Place under broiler, leaving broiler door open, and broil approximately 3 minutes per side, until nicely browned on the outside and still pink on the inside.

5. Transfer chops to dinner plates and remove strings.

Sautéed Red Peppers with Pancetta

6 red bell peppers (about 1½ pounds total weight)
3 large cloves garlic
¼ pound pancetta (about 5 slices), or 2 ounces bacon
1 tablespoon olive oil
2 tablespoons balsamic vinegar
2 teaspoons fresh oregano, left in small leaves,
    or 1 teaspoon dried
1 teaspoon freshly ground black pepper
Oregano leaves or parsley sprigs for garnish (optional)

1. Wash, dry, and halve peppers lengthwise. Core, seed, and derib. With chef's knife, cut into ¼-inch-wide strips.

2. Peel garlic and, using paring knife, cut into thin slivers.

3. Briefly heat large heavy-gauge skillet or sauté pan over medium-high heat. Add pancetta and sauté until crisp. Using slotted spoon, remove and drain on paper towels.

4. Return pan to heat. Add olive oil and pepper strips. Sauté over medium-high heat until peppers are heated through, about 1 minute. Add garlic slivers, stir, and cover pan. Reduce heat to low and cook until peppers are tender, about 20 minutes. Remove from heat.

5. Crumble pancetta and add half of it to peppers along with vinegar, oregano, and pepper. Toss to combine.

6. Divide peppers among dinner plates and garnish each serving with a sprinkling of the remaining pancetta and a few oregano leaves or parsley sprigs, if desired.

Pasta with Toasted Pine Nuts and Parmesan Cheese

1 tablespoon salt
1 tablespoon olive oil
2 ounces Parmesan cheese
4 tablespoons unsalted butter
¼ cup pine nuts
½ pound dry or fresh egg pasta, such as fettuccine

1. In large saucepan or stockpot, bring 4 quarts water, 1 tablespoon salt, and 1 tablespoon olive oil to a boil over medium heat.

2. Grate Parmesan cheese and set aside.

3. In small heavy-gauge skillet or sauté pan, melt butter over medium heat. When it foams, add pine nuts and cook, stirring, until both butter and pine nuts turn golden brown. Remove from heat. Using slotted spoon, transfer half the pine nuts to a small bowl or cup and reserve for garnish.

4. Add pasta to the boiling water. Cook dry pasta 8 to 12 minutes, fresh pasta 3 to 5 minutes, or until *al dente*.

5. Place colander over bowl and drain pasta into it: The pasta water will heat the bowl. Empty the bowl of water, dry with paper towel, and fill with pasta.

6. Toss pasta with the remaining pine nuts and all the browned butter from skillet. Add Parmesan cheese and toss again.

7. Place a portion of pasta on each plate and garnish with reserved pine nuts.

Jack Ubaldi

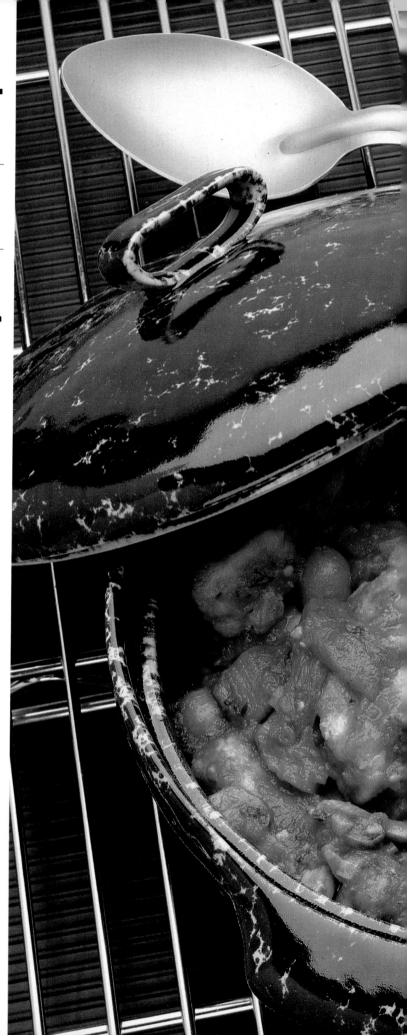

Following in his father's footsteps, Jack Ubaldi has become an accomplished butcher, and meat cutting is an art he now teaches. "When I handle meat, it is like a sculptor handling clay," he says. "I like to cut it into pleasing shapes and portions." He tells his students to prepare raw meat properly, so that it will look as appetizing as possible when cooked. Working with prime-grade meats, he can use lesser cuts to good advantage. Instead of using a T-bone steak, for example, he can use shoulder steak and still produce a delicious meal.

Although Jack Ubaldi has lived in New York for years, he still considers himself an Italian cook. When he assembles a meal, he follows the culinary traditions of his native region: a small amount of oil, mild cheeses, delicate seasonings, and lightly cooked meats and vegetables. For the main course of Menu 1, Jack Ubaldi combines a medley of vegetables with cubes of veal in a simple and delicious stew. As a side dish, he offers Italian-style zucchini rolls filled with an herbed mixture of cheese, meat, and tomatoes.

In Menu 2, the medallions of beef with fennel sauce (*bistecchi di manzo al finocchio*) was his mother's recipe. Fennel seeds, widely used in Italian cooking, impart a subtle anise flavor. The Menu 3 recipe for veal birds, which he devised many years ago, contains two well-known Italian foods: prosciutto and mozzarella cheese.

This Italian stew of veal cubes with an assortment of vegetables cooks in less than an hour. The stew and the zucchini roulades can both be served directly from their cookware. Italian bread is an appealing addition to this hearty meal.

Veal Mirelle Sauté, Italian Style
Zucchini Rolls

The cook prepares the veal Mirelle with several standard stew vegetables: carrots, onions, tomatoes, and mushrooms. As an unusual touch, he adds an eggplant.

For the zucchini rolls, select firm, bright green zucchini. Store them in a plastic bag in the refrigerator, where they keep for up to one week. Before slicing them, scrub them well to remove any grit.

WHAT TO DRINK

An Italian wine would be excellent with this menu. Choose a light, dry red, such as a young Chianti or a Barbera.

SHOPPING LIST AND STAPLES

1½ pounds boneless leg of veal, cut into 2-inch cubes
½ pound ground beef
2 small, straight zucchini (about ½ pound total weight)
Small eggplant
Medium-size carrot
½ pound mushrooms
Medium-size yellow onion
2 large cloves garlic
Small bunch fresh parsley
Small bunch fresh basil, or 1 teaspoon dried
1 egg
5 tablespoons unsalted butter
¼ pound Parmesan cheese
½ cup chicken stock, preferably homemade (see page 13), or canned
Two 16-ounce cans peeled plum tomatoes
1 teaspoon tomato paste
2¼-ounce jar pitted green olives
2 tablespoons olive oil, plus additional 2 tablespoons or 2 tablespoons vegetable oil
2 tablespoons flour
¼ teaspoon dried oregano
Salt and freshly ground pepper
½ cup dry white wine

UTENSILS

Food processor or blender (optional)
Large heavy-gauge skillet with ovenproof handle or cast-iron casserole, with cover
Medium-size skillet
9 x 12-inch cookie sheet
9-inch pie pan
Large bowl plus additional large bowl (if not using processor)
Medium-size bowl
Colander or sieve
Measuring cups and spoons
Chef's knife
Paring knife
Metal spatula
Wooden spatula
Slotted metal spoon
Grater
Pastry brush
Toothpicks

START-TO-FINISH STEPS

1. Grate cheese and chop herbs for zucchini rolls recipe.
2. Follow zucchini rolls recipe steps 1 through 3.
3. While zucchini bakes, follow veal recipe step 1.
4. Follow zucchini rolls recipe steps 4 through 6.
5. While zucchini rolls bake, follow veal recipe steps 2 through 12.
6. When veal has cooked a total of 30 minutes, complete recipe step 13 and serve with zucchini rolls.

RECIPES

Veal Mirelle Sauté, Italian Style

Small eggplant
Salt
Medium-size yellow onion
Medium-size carrot
2 large cloves garlic
2¼-ounce jar pitted green olives
1½ pounds boneless leg of veal
2 tablespoons flour
5 tablespoons unsalted butter
2 tablespoons olive oil
16-ounce can peeled plum tomatoes
½ cup dry white wine
½ cup chicken stock
1 teaspoon tomato paste
½ pound mushrooms
Freshly ground pepper

1. Peel eggplant and cut into 1-inch cubes. Sprinkle lightly with salt. Toss to distribute salt evenly, and set aside in sieve or colander.

2. With chef's knife, chop onion and finely chop carrot or, if using food processor or blender, process carrot 5 to 10 seconds. With flat of chef's knife, crush garlic. Remove peel and set aside. Drain olives.

3. On wax paper, toss veal lightly with flour.

4. In large skillet or casserole, heat 2 tablespoons each butter and oil over high heat. Add veal and sauté until browned, about 4 to 8 minutes. Using slotted metal spoon, transfer veal to large bowl and set aside.

5. Pour off all but 1 tablespoon fat from pan and add 1 tablespoon butter. Lower heat to medium-high. Add onion, carrot, and garlic, and cook, stirring with wooden spatula, about 3 minutes.

6. Remove garlic, return meat to pan, and cook, stirring frequently, over medium-high heat about 5 minutes.

7. While meat is cooking, drain tomatoes and cut into quarters.

8. Lower heat to medium, add wine to pan, and cook until evaporated, 8 to 10 minutes. Then add chicken stock, tomatoes, tomato paste, and olives. Cover and cook over very low heat, stirring 2 or 3 times, 30 minutes.

9. With damp paper towels, wipe mushrooms. If large, cut mushrooms into quarters.

10. In medium-size skillet, heat 1 tablespoon butter over medium-high heat. Add mushrooms, and sauté 5 minutes. Transfer mushrooms to bowl used for veal and set aside.

11. With paper towels, pat eggplant dry.

12. In skillet used for mushrooms, melt the remaining tablespoon butter, over medium-high heat. Add eggplant and sauté 5 minutes. Transfer eggplant to bowl with mushrooms and set aside.

13. When meat has cooked 30 minutes, add mushrooms and eggplant and cook 10 to 12 minutes, or until vegetables are crisp-tender. Season to taste with salt and pepper.

Zucchini Rolls

2 small, straight zucchini (about ½ pound total weight)
2 tablespoons olive or vegetable oil
½ pound ground beef
3 tablespoons grated Parmesan cheese
1 egg
Salt
Freshly ground pepper
16-ounce can peeled plum tomatoes
1 tablespoon finely chopped fresh basil, or 1 teaspoon dried
1 tablespoon finely chopped fresh parsley
¼ teaspoon dried oregano

1. Preheat oven to 425 degrees.

2. Wash zucchini well, dry with paper towels, and trim off ends. With chef's knife, cut zucchini lengthwise into 4 slices, about ⅛ to ¼ inch thick.

3. Lightly oil cookie sheet and arrange slices in a single layer. With basting brush, brush each slice with oil. Bake 8

to 10 minutes. Remove zucchini from oven and let cool. Leave oven on.

4. In medium-size bowl, combine ground beef, Parmesan, egg, and salt and pepper to taste. Form mixture into 8 small meatballs.

5. Place a meatball at one end of each slice of zucchini, roll up, and secure each roll with toothpicks. Place rolls in pie pan.

6. Drain tomatoes and purée in food processor or blender. Stir in basil, parsley, oregano, and salt and pepper to taste. Or, using chef's knife, finely chop tomatoes and combine them in large bowl with same ingredients. Pour mixture over zucchini rolls and bake 30 minutes.

ADDED TOUCH

For this quick but impressive dessert, the currants are first soaked in Cointreau or Grand Marnier, sweet orange-flavored French liqueurs, and then they and the bananas are flamed with either Cognac or brandy.

Bananas Flambé Cordon Bleu

1 tablespoon currants or raisins, coarsely chopped
¼ to ⅓ cup Cointreau, Grand Marnier, or any orange-flavored liqueur
2 tablespoons unsalted butter
2 tablespoons plus 1 teaspoon sugar
2 tablespoons flour (approximately)
4 firm bananas
2 oranges
1 lemon
½ teaspoon cornstarch
2 tablespoons Cognac or brandy

1. In small bowl, soak currants or raisins in 1 to 2 tablespoons liqueur.

2. Preheat oven to 400 degrees.

3. Butter pie pan and coat with 1 tablespoon sugar.

4. Place flour on wax paper; peel bananas and lightly coat with flour.

5. In large skillet, melt butter over medium heat. Add bananas and brown on all sides, turning with wooden spatula. Transfer bananas to prepared pie pan.

6. Sprinkle bananas with remaining sugar. Bake about 20 minutes, or until sugar melts.

7. While bananas cook, squeeze oranges and lemon through sieve to catch pits, and pour juice into small saucepan.

8. Drain currants or raisins and reserve liqueur. Add fruit to juice and bring to a boil over medium-high heat, then lower heat.

9. In small bowl or cup, combine cornstarch with ¼ cup cold water. Add to saucepan and simmer until mixture starts to thicken. Add reserved liqueur and keep mixture at a low simmer until bananas are ready.

10. Remove bananas from oven and pour sauce over them. Add Cognac or brandy and, averting face, carefully set aflame. When flames have died, serve.

Tomatoes and Mozzarella
Medallions of Beef with Fennel Sauce
Neapolitan-Style Zucchini and Baby Carrots

The tomato, basil, olive, mozzarella, and anchovy platter is an appetizing prelude to the beef medallions and vegetables.

The sliced tomatoes and mozzarella cheese antipasto platter includes slightly bitter, oil-cured Greek or Italian black olives, available at most supermarkets. These olives are quite different in flavor and texture from the brine-packed California olives. Together with the anchovies, capers, and fresh basil, they give this dish an Italian touch.

WHAT TO DRINK

An Italian Cabernet or a simple Châteauneuf du Pape would be the best choices.

SHOPPING LIST AND STAPLES

4 slices filet mignon (about 6 ounces each)
Large onion
¾ pound baby carrots
2 medium-size zucchini (about 1 pound total weight)
1 head Boston or 2 heads Bibb lettuce
3 ripe plum tomatoes
2 large beefsteak tomatoes (about 1 pound total weight)
Small bunch fresh basil
Small bunch fresh parsley
Small bunch fresh oregano, or ½ teaspoon dried

Large clove garlic
4 tablespoons unsalted butter
½ pound fresh mozzarella
½ cup beef stock, preferably homemade (see page 13), or canned
1 tablespoon tomato paste
2-ounce tin rolled anchovies with capers
4 ounces oil-cured black olives
4 tablespoons olive oil
4 tablespoons flour
1 teaspoon fennel seeds
Pinch of red pepper flakes
Salt and freshly ground black pepper
½ cup Marsala or dry sherry
½ cup dry red wine

UTENSILS

2 large skillets, one with heatproof cover
Medium-size saucepan
Heatproof casserole with cover
Heatproof platter
Colander
Salad spinner (optional)
Measuring cups and spoons
Chef's knife
Paring knife
Wooden spoon
Wooden spatula
Metal tongs

START-TO-FINISH STEPS

1. Follow zucchini and carrots recipe step 1.
2. Follow tomatoes recipe steps 1 through 4.
3. Follow zucchini and carrots recipe steps 2 through 4.
4. Follow medallions recipe steps 1 through 4.
5. Serve tomato and mozzarella salad.
6. Follow medallions recipe step 5, zucchini and carrots recipe step 5, and serve.

RECIPES

Tomatoes and Mozzarella

1 head Boston or 2 heads Bibb lettuce
2 large beefsteak tomatoes (about 1 pound total weight)
4 to 8 sprigs basil
½ pound fresh mozzarella, cut into 8 slices
24 oil-cured black olives (about 4 ounces)
4 rolled anchovies with capers

1. Rinse lettuce leaves and dry in salad spinner or pat dry with paper towels. Divide leaves among 4 individual plates. Wash and dry tomatoes and basil sprigs.
2. With chef's knife, cut tomatoes into ½-inch-thick slices and arrange on lettuce. Place mozzarella over tomatoes.
3. Arrange olives around tomatoes and cheese, and place 1 rolled anchovy on each serving.

4. Garnish each serving with a sprig or two of basil. Cover plates loosely and set aside until ready to serve.

Medallions of Beef with Fennel Sauce

4 tablespoons flour
4 slices filet mignon (about 6 ounces each)
2 tablespoons unsalted butter
½ cup Marsala or dry sherry
½ cup dry red wine
½ cup beef stock
1 teaspoon fennel seeds
1 tablespoon tomato paste
Salt and freshly ground pepper

1. Lightly flour filets. In large skillet, heat butter over medium high heat. Add meat and sauté 3 minutes on each side, or until browned.
2. With tongs, remove filets from skillet, transfer to heat-proof platter, and keep warm in 200-degree oven.
3. Add Marsala to skillet and, stirring continuously, deglaze pan over high heat until liquid is reduced by half. Add red wine, stock, fennel, and tomato paste. Simmer until reduced by half. Add salt and pepper to taste.
4. Return meat to skillet and cook in sauce over medium-high heat 2 minutes. Cover skillet and keep warm in oven.
5. Transfer filets to warm plates and nap with sauce.

Neapolitan-Style Zucchini and Baby Carrots

¾ pound baby carrots, peeled
Salt
2 medium-size zucchini, sliced into ¼-inch-thick rounds
Large onion, peeled and sliced
Large clove garlic, peeled and crushed
3 ripe plum tomatoes, peeled, seeded, and quartered
4 tablespoons olive oil
1½ teaspoons fresh oregano, or ½ teaspoon dried
Pinch of red pepper flakes
2 tablespoons unsalted butter
Freshly ground pepper
1 to 2 tablespoons chopped fresh parsley

1. Preheat oven to 200 degrees. In saucepan bring carrots with cold water to cover and a pinch of salt to a boil over high heat. Reduce heat and simmer carrots until tender, about 20 minutes.
2. In large skillet, heat oil over medium-high heat. Add garlic to skillet and sauté until lightly browned. Remove garlic and discard. Add onions and cook, stirring with wooden spatula, 2 to 3 minutes. Stir in zucchini.
3. Season mixture with oregano, red pepper flakes, and salt to taste. Add tomatoes and cook until vegetables are just tender, approximately 4 minutes. Lower heat just to keep vegetables warm.
4. In colander, drain carrots. Return them to saucepan with butter and pepper to taste. Add zucchini mixture and toss. Transfer mixture to ovenproof casserole, cover, and keep warm in oven.
5. When ready to serve, sprinkle with parsley.

Veal Birds Milanese
Braised Celery

Arrange the skewered veal birds and prosciutto on lettuce leaves, and garnish them with chopped parsley. Serve the braised celery hearts, topped with melted cheese and crumbled bacon, on the side.

I n this menu, the veal cutlets are pounded thin and then wrapped around a stuffing of bread crumbs, egg yolks, chicken livers, and prosciutto. Prosciutto, a raw, un-smoked, air-dried Italian ham, is deep pink, moist, and not overly salty. Buy prosciutto at Italian groceries or at the delicatessen counter of a supermarket. If you cannot find it, substitute Westphalian ham or a mild cured ham.

WHAT TO DRINK

First choice is a Chianti Classico Riserva. Good alternatives would be a California Cabernet or Burgundy.

SHOPPING LIST AND STAPLES

8 slices veal cutlet (about 1½ pounds total weight), pounded thin
8 slices prosciutto (about ¼ pound total weight)
3 chicken livers (about ¼ pound total weight)
5 slices bacon (about ¼ pound)
1 head Boston lettuce
2 heads celery
Small onion
1 clove garlic
4 large whole fresh sage leaves, or ¼ teaspoon dried
Small bunch fresh parsley
2 eggs
4 tablespoons unsalted butter
¼ pound mozzarella
2 slices Swiss cheese or provolone (about 3 ounces)
½ cup beef stock, preferably homemade (see page 13), or canned
½ cup chicken stock, preferably homemade (see page 13), or canned
2 tablespoons olive oil
3 tablespoons unseasoned bread crumbs
Pinch of dried marjoram
Pinch of dried sage
Pinch of dried basil
Salt and freshly ground pepper
½ cup Marsala or dry sherry
½ cup dry white wine

UTENSILS

Food processor or blender (optional)
Large skillet with cover

Medium-size skillet with cover
Small skillet
Medium-size saucepan
8 x 8 x 2-inch ovenproof baking dish
Large bowl (if not using food processor)
Colander
Salad spinner (optional)
Measuring cups and spoons
Chef's knife
Paring knife
Wooden spatula
Garlic press (optional)
Four 8-inch metal or bamboo skewers
Toothpicks

START-TO-FINISH STEPS

At least 30 minutes ahead: If using bamboo skewers, soak them in water until needed, to reduce charring.

1. Follow celery recipe steps 1 through 7.
2. While celery is cooking, chop parsley and separate eggs for veal recipe. Follow veal recipe steps 1 through 6.
3. Follow celery recipe step 8 and veal recipe steps 7 through 9.
4. Follow celery recipe steps 9 and 10, veal recipe step 10, and serve.

RECIPES

Veal Birds Milanese

1 head Boston lettuce
3 tablespoons unsalted butter
3 chicken livers (about ¼ pound total weight)
3 tablespoons unseasoned bread crumbs
2 teaspoons chopped fresh parsley
2 egg yolks
8 slices prosciutto (about ¼ pound total weight)
¼ pound mozzarella
Salt and freshly ground pepper
8 slices veal cutlet, pounded thin
4 large whole fresh sage leaves, or ¼ teaspoon dried
2 tablespoons olive oil
½ cup Marsala or dry sherry
½ cup beef stock

1. Wash lettuce leaves and dry in salad spinner or pat dry with paper towels. Refrigerate until ready to use.
2. Remove membranes from livers. In small skillet, melt 1 tablespoon butter over medium-high heat. Add livers and sauté 2 minutes. Remove pan from heat.
3. In food processor or blender, process bread crumbs, 2 teaspoons parsley, egg yolks, and 4 slices prosciutto briefly to mix. Add livers and process about 10 seconds. Or finely chop prosciutto and livers first, and then combine them in large bowl with same ingredients. Set aside.
4. With chef's knife, cut mozzarella into small cubes. Lightly salt and pepper veal cutlets.

5. Place about 3 rounded teaspoons chicken-liver stuffing and a few mozzarella cubes in center of each cutlet. Roll up cutlets, tucking in ends. Secure birds with toothpicks.
6. On each skewer, put 2 birds, separated by a slice of the remaining prosciutto and a sage leaf.
7. In large skillet, heat oil and the remaining butter over high heat. Add birds and brown quickly on all sides, about 5 minutes. Reduce heat to medium-high.
8. Remove skillet from heat and drain off excess butter and oil. Add Marsala, return pan to heat, and increase heat slowly. Cook, stirring, until liquid is reduced to less than half, about 2 to 3 minutes.
9. Add beef stock. Cover skillet and simmer over low heat 10 minutes.
10. When ready to serve, divide lettuce among 4 plates and top each with veal bird skewer. Remove toothpicks.

Braised Celery

2 heads celery
Salt
1 small onion
1 clove garlic
5 slices bacon (about ¼ pound)
1 tablespoon unsalted butter
Pinch of dried marjoram
Pinch of dried sage
Pinch of dried basil
Freshly ground pepper
½ cup dry white wine
½ cup chicken stock
2 slices Swiss cheese or provolone (about 3 ounces)

1. Remove outer stalks from celery heads and reserve for another use. Wash celery hearts.
2. In medium-size saucepan, bring celery hearts with water almost to cover and pinch of salt to a boil. Lower heat and simmer 8 minutes. In colander, drain hearts and refresh under cold water. Pat dry with paper towels.
3. Peel and chop onion. Peel garlic and crush in garlic press or mince finely. Set aside.
4. In medium-size skillet, fry 2 bacon slices until crisp. Drain on paper towel, crumble, and set aside. Pour off bacon fat. Add butter to skillet and cook the remaining bacon over medium-high heat 2 minutes. Add onion and sauté until translucent.
5. Cut celery hearts in half. Add celery hearts, garlic, marjoram, sage, basil, and pepper to skillet, shaking pan to mix. Turn heat to high.
6. Add white wine and bring to a boil. Reduce heat and simmer to reduce wine to less than half.
7. Add chicken stock and return to a boil. Lower heat and simmer, covered, 30 minutes. Slice cheese into strips.
8. About 10 minutes before celery hearts will be done, preheat oven to 350 degrees.
9. Transfer celery heart mixture to baking dish. Arrange cheese strips over celery hearts.
10. Bake just until cheese is melted but not browned, about 4 to 5 minutes. Top with crumbled bacon and serve.

Mary Beth Clark

After extensive research on American cuisine, Mary Beth Clark reports that the quintessential American meal—steak and potatoes—is far from passé. But people now tend to trim portion sizes and to prefer leaner beef, shorter cooking times, and unusual sauces. To balance meals, cooks serve more vegetables as side dishes.

In line with these observations, Mary Beth Clark has created three contemporary beef menus by updating some French classics:

Menu 1, a summer meal, is a variation on the theme of *boeuf à la ficelle*, or French boiled beef: here, the meat, a center cut of tenderloin sometimes marketed as beef loin tenderloin roast, is gently poached and served rare and juicy. It is accompanied by béarnaise sauce, a close relative of the egg-yolk-and-butter-rich Hollandaise but flavored with shallots, tarragon, and vinegar instead of lemon juice.

Menu 2, *tournedos*, the French term for thick steaks cut from the filet mignon portion nearest to the center of the tenderloin, are filled with blue-cheese butter and served with braised, garlic-scented escarole and crostini, an adaptation of Italian fried bread.

The third menu features *entrecôte*, the French equivalent of our rib steak, highlighted here with the woodsy flavor of wild mushrooms in a light Madeira sauce and flanked by three vegetable side dishes.

In these menus, as in all of Mary Beth Clark's recipes, a key role is played by fresh herbs and seasonal vegetables cooked briefly to retain nutrients.

A good hot-weather entrée, this beef tenderloin, which is prepared according to a French method and served with béarnaise sauce, is best served warm. The julienned lemon zest used to garnish the asparagus also enhances its flavor.

75

Medallions of Rare Tenderloin à la Ficelle
Steamed Asparagus with Lemon and Chive Butter
Vegetable and Rice Salad with Creamy Garlic Vinaigrette

The term "à la ficelle," literally "of the string" or "on a string," describes a classic French cooking method in which a piece of meat is suspended in boiling broth by a string or in cheesecloth to prevent it from touching the bottom and sides of the pot and forming a tough brown crust. The result is moister, more tender meat. This adaptation calls for the center cut of tenderloin, the choicest and most expensive cut of the steer, and for poaching rather than boiling.

WHAT TO DRINK

Although asparagus can be a difficult partner for wines, the beef and its sauce go well with a relatively full-bodied and flavorful red wine like a St. Emilion or a Merlot.

SHOPPING LIST AND STAPLES

1¾ pounds chateaubriand (beef loin tenderloin roast)
1 pound asparagus
Small bunch celery
Large carrot
Small red bell pepper
3 fresh plum tomatoes
Small bunch scallions
Medium-size lemon
2 large shallots
2 small cloves garlic
Small bunch fresh parsley
Small bunch fresh chives
Small bunch fresh tarragon, or 1 teaspoon dried
Small bunch fresh summer savory, or 1 teaspoon dried
Small bunch fresh thyme, or ½ teaspoon dried
3 eggs
½ pint heavy cream
2 sticks plus 3 tablespoons unsalted butter
5 cups beef broth, preferably homemade (see page 13), or canned
16-ounce jar Calamata black olives or 7¼-ounce can California black olives
3½-ounce jar capers
4½ tablespoons cold-pressed virgin olive oil
2½ tablespoons red wine vinegar
5 teaspoons white wine vinegar, plus additional 1¼ teaspoons if not using balsamic and sherry vinegars
1 teaspoon balsamic vinegar (optional)
¼ teaspoon sherry vinegar (optional)

1 cup long-grain white rice
Small bay leaf
Salt and freshly ground white pepper

UTENSILS

2 large saucepans
Medium-size saucepan
Small saucepan
Vegetable steamer
Plate
Large bowl
Medium-size bowl
Small bowl
Strainer
Measuring cups and spoons
Chef's knife
Paring knife
Slotted spoon
Wooden spoon
Whisk
Zester
Kitchen string

START-TO-FINISH STEPS

1. Follow salad recipe step 1.
2. Follow tenderloin recipe steps 1 through 4.
3. Follow salad recipe step 2.
4. Follow béarnaise sauce recipe step 1 and asparagus recipe steps 1 and 2.
5. Follow tenderloin recipe step 5 and salad recipe steps 3 through 5.
6. Follow asparagus recipe step 3.
7. While asparagus are steaming, follow béarnaise sauce recipe step 2 and keep warm.
8. Remove asparagus from steamer and follow asparagus recipe step 4.
9. Follow salad recipe step 6, asparagus recipe step 5, tenderloin recipe step 6, and serve.

RECIPES

Medallions of Rare Tenderloin à la Ficelle

Large shallot
Small clove garlic

1 stalk celery
Large carrot
1 teaspoon chopped fresh thyme, or ½ teaspoon dried
6 parsley sprigs, stripped of leaves
1¾ pounds chateaubriand (beef loin tenderloin roast)
5 cups beef stock (approximately)
½ small bay leaf
Béarnaise sauce (see following recipe)

1. Peel shallot, garlic, celery, and carrot. Trim and quarter celery and carrot.
2. Tie string around tenderloin, leaving a long loop, so string can be put over handle of saucepan. The string should be long enough to submerge the tenderloin in the stock without meat touching pan.
3. In large saucepan, combine 5 cups water, beef stock, shallot, garlic, celery, carrot, bay leaf, thyme, and parsley leaves. Bring to a boil over high heat.
4. Suspend tenderloin in poaching liquid, so that meat is entirely immersed. Add additional hot stock or water if necessary. Over high heat, return to a boil and boil 3 minutes, until meat has lost its raw pink color. Reduce to a simmer, and poach, uncovered, 15 minutes for rare, 20 minutes for medium, and 25 minutes for well done.
5. With slotted spoon, remove meat and untie string. Drain meat and let rest 15 minutes to distribute juices.
6. Slice meat, divide among individual plates, and serve with béarnaise sauce.

Béarnaise Sauce

Large shallot, peeled and finely minced
2 teaspoons chopped fresh tarragon, or 1 teaspoon dried
2 teaspoons chopped fresh summer savory, or 1 teaspoon dried
2½ tablespoons red wine vinegar
Pinch of freshly ground white pepper
3 egg yolks
1 stick plus 4 tablespoons frozen unsalted butter
Salt

1. In medium-size saucepan used to cook rice for salad recipe, combine shallot, tarragon, summer savory, vinegar, and pepper. Reduce to thick paste over medium heat, about 2 minutes. While mixture is reducing, cut frozen butter into 1-tablespoon pieces.
2. Beat egg yolks with 1 tablespoon cold water. Remove saucepan from heat and whisk in yolks until well blended. Over low heat, whisk mixture constantly until thick, 30 to 60 seconds. Immediately add 2 tablespoons butter and whisk until almost completely melted. Add another tablespoon butter and again whisk until almost completely melted. If necessary, control heat by sliding pan on and off burner. Continue until all butter is incorporated. Or, in food processor or blender, gradually incorporate butter into mixture. The sauce should be a thick, creamy yellow. (If sauce separates, immediately remove from heat and whisk in 1 to 2 tablespoons cold tap water.) Add salt to taste.

Steamed Asparagus with Lemon and Chive Butter

Medium-size lemon
1 pound asparagus, washed and trimmed
6 tablespoons unsalted butter
3 tablespoons freshly snipped chives
Salt and freshly ground white pepper

1. Cut strips of lemon zest and slice enough into thin julienne to measure 2 teaspoons.
2. In large saucepan, bring 2 inches water to a boil over high heat; water level should not reach vegetable steamer.
3. In steamer, steam asparagus until barely tender, 4 to 12 minutes. Cooking time will vary with size of spears.
4. In small saucepan, melt butter over medium-low heat. Add chives and lemon zest. Season to taste with salt and white pepper.
5. Divide asparagus among individual plates and drizzle with lemon and chive butter.

Vegetable and Rice Salad with Creamy Garlic Vinaigrette

1 cup long-grain white rice
1 tablespoon unsalted butter
2 tablespoons capers
½ cup chopped seeded plum tomatoes
¼ cup chopped pitted Calamata black olives, preferably, or California black olives
¼ cup diced red bell pepper
2 tablespoons minced scallions
Salt and freshly ground white pepper
5 teaspoons white wine vinegar, plus additional 1¼ teaspoons if not using balsamic and sherry vinegars
1 teaspoon balsamic vinegar (optional)
¼ teaspoon sherry vinegar (optional)
¼ teaspoon minced garlic
4½ tablespoons cold-pressed virgin olive oil
5 teaspoons heavy cream (at room temperature)

1. In medium-size saucepan, combine 1⅓ cups water, rice, and butter. Bring to a boil over medium-high heat and continue boiling 1 minute, scraping bottom and sides of pan with wooden spoon to prevent sticking. Reduce heat to low, cover, and cook until rice is tender, 18 to 20 minutes, stirring occasionally. Drain rice in strainer, spread on plate, and cool in refrigerator.
2. Rinse capers, if salt-packed, and pat dry with paper towel. If vinegar-packed, drain.
3. When rice is cool, transfer to large bowl and add tomatoes, olives, red pepper, scallions, capers, and salt and pepper to taste. Toss.
4. In medium-size bowl, combine vinegars and garlic. In slow, steady stream add olive oil, whisking to combine. In same manner, add heavy cream. Season to taste with salt and pepper.
5. Pour vinaigrette over rice and vegetables and toss well. Refrigerate until ready to serve.
6. Divide salad among individual plates.

Tournedos with Blue Cheese Butter
Crostini with Shallot-Parsley Topping
Braised Escarole

Thick tenderloin steaks, known as *tournedos*, are cut from the center portion of the tenderloin. The French often stuff *tournedos* with the liver of a specially fattened breed of goose and serve them on fried bread. Instead, Mary Beth Clark stuffs these steaks with a rich butter made from blue cheese and serves the fried, herbed bread on the side. Blue cheeses can be sharp in flavor; use Roquefort to give a milder taste. Serve half the blue cheese butter as an accompaniment.

Crostini, Italian fried bread or polenta topped with

Blue cheese or Roquefort butter is the stuffing here for tournedos of beef. The assertive flavor of the filling is balanced by crostini with a shallot and parsley topping and escarole braised with garlic.

savory spreads, frequently appear as an hors d'oeuvre in Italy. Use day-old bread for this recipe (or bread that has been dried in the oven), since fresh bread absorbs too much oil when fried.

Escarole is a curly-leaf green of the endive family. If it is not available, buy fresh spinach or curly endive (chicory). Braising, the cooking method used for this dish, is a good way to use leftover salad greens before they wilt.

WHAT TO DRINK

The cook suggests a robust California Cabernet Sauvignon or Zinfandel to balance the assertive flavors of this menu.

Four 8-ounce *tournedos* (steaks cut from filet mignon portion nearest center of tenderloin), each about 1½ inches thick
Medium-size head escarole (about 1½ pounds)
1 red bell pepper (optional)
Small bunch scallions
2 shallots
6 cloves garlic
Small bunch fresh chives
Small bunch fresh thyme, or ¼ teaspoon dried
Small bunch fresh parsley
1 stick plus 3½ tablespoons unsalted butter
3 ounces blue cheese or Roquefort
1 cup plus 2½ tablespoons cold-pressed virgin olive oil
1 tablespoon Dijon mustard
Small, long Italian loaf (6 to 8 ounces), preferably 1 day old
Whole allspice
Pinch of Cayenne pepper (optional)
Salt
Freshly ground white pepper
Freshly ground black pepper
3 tablespoons dry vermouth

UTENSILS

Food processor or blender
Large skillet
Medium-size skillet with cover
Large sauté pan
Small saucepan
2 small bowls
Salad spinner (optional)
Measuring cups and spoons
Chef's knife
Paring knife
Bread knife (optional)
2 metal spatulas
Rubber spatula
Slotted spoon
Cake rack
Mortar and pestle or rolling pin
Deep-fat thermometer

START-TO-FINISH STEPS

1. Using mortar and pestle or rolling pin, pulverize enough allspice to measure 2 pinches for tournedos and crostini recipes. Follow crostini recipe steps 1 through 3.

2. Follow tournedos recipe steps 1 through 3.
3. Follow escarole recipe steps 1 through 5.
4. While escarole simmers, follow tournedos recipe step 4.
5. While tournedos are cooking, follow crostini recipe step 4.
6. Follow tournedos recipe steps 5 and 6, crostini recipe step 5, escarole recipe step 6, and serve.

RECIPES

Tournedos with Blue Cheese Butter

Four 8-ounce *tournedos* (steaks cut from filet mignon portion nearest center of tenderloin), each about 1½ inches thick
1 clove garlic
½ red bell pepper for garnish (optional)
3 ounces blue cheese or Roquefort
6½ tablespoons unsalted butter
Pinch of freshly ground allspice
Pinch of Cayenne pepper (optional)
2 teaspoons freshly snipped chives
1 teaspoon minced fresh thyme, or ¼ teaspoon dried, plus 4 fresh sprigs for garnish (optional)
1½ tablespoons cold-pressed virgin olive oil
Salt
Freshly ground black pepper

1. Using chef's knife, butterfly each tournedos by slicing horizontally through middle of steak to make a "book," leaving ½-inch "hinge." Set aside uncovered at room temperature.
2. Peel and mince enough garlic to measure ⅛ teaspoon. If using, wash, core, seed, and halve pepper. Cut one half lengthwise into ¼-inch strips and set aside. Reserve remaining half for other use.
3. In food processor or blender, combine cheese, 5 tablespoons butter, garlic, allspice, and Cayenne, if using, and blend until smooth. Transfer mixture to small bowl and, using rubber spatula, blend in chives and thyme. Refrigerate until needed.
4. In large sauté pan, heat oil and remaining 1½ tablespoons butter over medium heat until butter has melted. Turn heat to high and sear each tournedos all over, opening "hinge" to sear inside. Using 2 metal spatulas, tilt each tournedos to sear any raw edges, being careful not to pierce meat. Close up tournedos, reduce heat to medium, and continue to cook 1 to 2 minutes per side for rare, 3 to 4 minutes per side for medium, and 5 to 6 minutes per side for well done.
5. Remove blue cheese butter from refrigerator and divide in half. Reserve one half for garnish and divide other half into 4 uniform-size portions. Working quickly, open tournedos and spoon a portion of blue cheese butter into center of each. Close tournedos and sprinkle with salt and pepper to taste.
6. Transfer tournedos to individual dinner plates. Garnish each with a slice of red pepper and a sprig of thyme, if desired, and accompany with crostini. Serve remaining blue cheese butter on the side.

Crostini with Shallot-Parsley Topping

Small, long Italian loaf (6 to 8 ounces), preferably 1 day old
2 tablespoons chopped shallots
½ teaspoon chopped garlic
3 tablespoons dry vermouth
4 tablespoons unsalted butter
¼ cup coarsely chopped parsley
1 tablespoon Dijon mustard
Pinch of freshly ground allspice
Freshly ground white pepper
1 cup cold-pressed virgin olive oil

1. With bread knife or chef's knife, slice loaf diagonally into eight ¾-inch-thick slices. Arrange slices in a single layer on rack in cold oven or leave on cake rack at room temperature to dry out bread.
2. Peel and chop shallots and garlic.
3. In small saucepan, combine shallots, garlic, and vermouth. Bring to a boil and simmer over low heat until vermouth has evaporated, about 4 minutes. Remove from heat and cool. Cut butter into 8 pieces. In food processor or blender, combine vermouth mixture, butter, parsley, mustard, allspice, and pepper to taste. Blend 5 to 10 seconds. Refrigerate mixture until needed.
4. In large skillet, heat oil to 325 degrees on deep-fat thermometer. Add 4 bread slices and fry until golden on each side, about 20 seconds on first side and 15 seconds on second. Remove slices with slotted spoon and drain on paper-towel-lined cake rack. Repeat with remaining slices.
5. Spread crostini with shallot-parsley topping and serve with tournedos.

Braised Escarole

Medium-size head escarole (about 1½ pounds)
8 scallions
1 tablespoon unsalted butter
1 tablespoon cold-pressed virgin olive oil
4 cloves garlic

1. Wash escarole and dry in salad spinner or pat dry with paper towels. Cut, across leaves, into 2-inch-wide strips.
2. Wash and trim scallions. Cut crosswise into ¼-inch pieces. Peel garlic and thinly slice enough to measure 4 teaspoons.
3. In medium-size skillet, heat butter and oil over medium heat. When butter is melted, sauté scallions and garlic 15 seconds, or just until they begin to become fragrant. Do not let garlic brown or it will turn bitter.
4. Add escarole and sauté just until limp, about 1 to 2 minutes.
5. Turn heat to low, cover, and simmer escarole until barely soft, about 3 to 4 minutes. If pan becomes dry, add 1 tablespoon water. When escarole is done, cover to keep warm.
6. Divide escarole, garlic, and scallions among individual salad plates.

Entrecôtes Forestière with Madeira Sauce
Sautéed Scallions / Steamed Buttered Carrots
New Potatoes with Shallots and Thyme

Because you need small, tender carrots and new potatoes, this menu is most appropriate for spring and early summer.

Arrange the steaks, topped with the mushroom and Madeira sauce, on a platter along with the sautéed scallions.

The entrecôte, or boneless beef rib eye steak, is a succulent, well-marbled cut. The recipe for Forestière (literally, in the manner of the forest) sauce calls for *cèpes*, also known as *porcini*, the large meaty brown mushrooms that grow wild under pine and other evergreen trees. Reconstitute these dried mushrooms by steeping them in a small amount of very hot water for 15 to 20 minutes. Then drain them and pat dry before using. Most food specialty shops and many supermarkets carry packaged cèpes, at one time an exotic ingredient. However, if you cannot locate them, the cook suggests other cultivated or wild mushroom alternates: chanterelles, morels, *shiitake*, and oyster mushrooms. Although usable, the cultivated white mushroom lacks the earthy flavor that, combined with Madeira (a distinctive fortified wine from Portugal), gives this sauce its character. Mary Beth Clark's recipe calls for Malmsey, a dark, sweetish Madeira (sometimes labeled golden Madeira) that can also be served as an aperitif or as a dessert wine. If you have difficulty finding Malmsey, you may use another Madeira, but the results will be different.

Although normally used as a garnish, scallions appear as a vegetable in this menu. They are sautéed briefly in butter to bring out their special sweet flavor.

Red Bliss potatoes, the young boiling variety often referred to as "new," are one of the most flavorful varieties of potato. They are lower in calories than noodles or rice and are good sources of a variety of nutrients. The potatoes and young carrots are steamed quickly to retain maximum texture, flavor, and nutrients. They can be cooked together in the same steamer, if desired.

WHAT TO DRINK

This classic menu calls for classic wines: a good Bordeaux or a fine California Cabernet.

SHOPPING LIST AND STAPLES

Two 14-ounce boneless rib eye steaks (entrecôtes), each about 1½ inches thick
4 medium-size red boiling potatoes, preferably Red Bliss (about 1 pound total weight)
¾ pound baby carrots
8 large shallots
2 large bunches scallions
Medium-size bunch parsley
Small bunch fresh thyme, or 1 teaspoon dried
1 stick plus 4 tablespoons unsalted butter
6 tablespoons salted butter
⅔ cup beef stock, preferably homemade (see page 13), or canned
1½ tablespoons virgin olive oil
1 ounce dried cèpes, or ¼ pound cultivated fresh mushrooms or edible wild mushrooms
Whole allspice
Salt

Freshly ground white pepper
Freshly ground black pepper
¼ cup Madeira, preferably Malmsey
¼ cup plus 1 tablespoon dry red wine

UTENSILS

Large heavy-gauge skillet
Medium-size heavy-gauge heatproof skillet
Large sauté pan
1 large saucepan with cover
Medium-size saucepan
Ovenproof platter
Small bowl
Vegetable steamer
Measuring cups and spoons
Chef's knife
Paring knife
2 metal spatulas
Wooden spatula
Wooden spoon
Whisk
Vegetable peeler
Mortar and pestle or rolling pin

START-TO-FINISH STEPS

At least 30 minutes ahead: For Madeira sauce, cut salted butter in six 1-tablespoon pieces, wrap in wax paper, and place in freezer.

1. Follow Madeira sauce recipe step 1. Peel and mince enough shallots to measure ½ cup for Madeira sauce and potatoes recipes.
2. Follow carrots recipe steps 1 through 3 and potatoes recipe steps 1 and 2, cooking both vegetables together in same pan.
3. While vegetables are steaming, follow entrecôtes recipe steps 1 and 2, and Madeira sauce recipe steps 2 and 3.
4. Follow scallions recipe step 1 and potatoes recipe step 3.
5. Follow entrecôtes recipe step 3.
6. Follow Madeira sauce recipe steps 4 through 6.
7. While sauce reduces, follow potatoes recipe step 4, carrots recipe step 4, scallions recipe step 2, and keep vegetables warm until ready to serve.
8. Follow Madeira sauce recipe step 7, entrecôtes recipe step 4, and serve with potatoes and carrots.

RECIPES

Entrecôtes Forestière with Madeira Sauce

Two 14-ounce boneless rib eye steaks (entrecôtes), each about 1½ inches thick
½ teaspoon freshly ground black pepper
1½ tablespoons cold-pressed virgin olive oil
1½ tablespoons unsalted butter
Madeira sauce (see following recipe)
Sautéed scallions (see following recipe)

1. Cut each entrecôte in half to make 4 entrecôtes. Sprinkle with black pepper on both sides. Set aside uncovered at room temperature.
2. Preheat oven to 200 degrees.
3. Heat large sauté pan over medium-high heat until hot. Add oil and butter and heat until butter is melted. Turn heat to high, place entrecôtes in pan, and sear until both sides have rich brown crust, about 1 minute per side. Using 2 metal spatulas, tilt each entrecôte and sear any raw edges. Do not pierce meat. Reduce heat to medium and continue to cook 1 minute per side for rare, 3 minutes per side for medium, and 5 minutes per side for well done. Transfer entrecôtes to ovenproof serving platter and keep warm in preheated oven until ready to serve.
4. Remove entrecôtes from oven. Serve either whole or thinly sliced, with a few tablespoons Madeira sauce spooned over each serving. Garnish with sautéed scallions.

Madeira Sauce

1 ounce dried cèpes, or ¼ pound fresh cultivated
    mushrooms or edible wild mushrooms
Whole allspice
1½ tablespoons unsalted butter
¼ cup minced shallots
¼ cup Madeira, preferably Malmsey
¼ cup plus 1 tablespoon dry red wine
⅔ cup beef stock
6 tablespoons frozen salted butter
Salt and freshly ground white pepper

1. Rinse dried cèpes, if using, and soak in small bowl with hot water to cover, 15 to 20 minutes, or until soft.
2. Using a mortar and pestle or rolling pin, pulverize enough whole allspice to measure a pinch.
3. Drain cèpes, pat dry with paper towels, and chop coarsely. Or, if using fresh mushrooms, wipe clean with damp paper towels and slice.
4. Pour off juices from sauté pan used for entrecôtes. Add 1½ tablespoons unsalted butter and melt over medium heat. Add shallots and sauté until barely soft and translucent, about 1 minute. Add cèpes or mushrooms and stir to combine.
5. Turn heat to high. Add Madeira and red wine, and deglaze pan, vigorously scraping up any brown bits clinging to bottom. Reduce liquid until you can no longer smell alcohol, about 15 seconds. Lower heat to medium.
6. Add beef stock and reduce liquid, stirring frequently, to ½ cup, about 4 to 5 minutes.
7. Remove pan from heat. Remove salted butter from freezer. Whisk frozen butter into sauce, 1 tablespoon at a time, until butter is incorporated and sauce is thick and smooth. Add a pinch of allspice and salt and pepper to taste.

Sautéed Scallions

16 scallions
1½ tablespoons unsalted butter

Salt
Freshly ground white pepper

1. Rinse scallions and pat dry with paper towels. Cut off roots and green portions about an inch above the point where they separate from the bulb. Discard.
2. In medium-size skillet, heat butter over medium heat until melted. Add scallions and sauté until barely tender, about 2 to 3 minutes. Season to taste with salt and pepper. Keep warm in 200-degree oven until ready to serve.

Steamed Buttered Carrots

¾ pound baby carrots
2 tablespoons unsalted butter
Salt
Freshly ground white pepper
Parsley sprigs for garnish (optional)

1. In saucepan large enough to accommodate vegetable steamer, bring water to a boil over high heat.
2. Rinse, peel, and trim carrots.
3. Place carrots with potatoes (see following recipe) in vegetable steamer set in saucepan, cover, and steam over high heat until tender, about 10 to 12 minutes. (Water level must not reach steamer.) Remove pan from heat, uncover, and cool slightly.
4. In large skillet, heat butter over medium-low heat until melted. Add carrots, toss with wooden spatula to coat, and season to taste with salt and pepper. Transfer to heatproof serving bowl and keep warm in 200-degree oven until ready to serve.

New Potatoes with Shallots and Thyme

4 medium-size red boiling potatoes, preferably Red Bliss
    (about 1 pound total weight)
6 tablespoons unsalted butter
¼ cup minced shallots
½ cup chopped fresh parsley
1 tablespoon chopped fresh thyme, or 1 teaspoon dried
Salt
Freshly ground white pepper

1. In large saucepan, bring water to a boil over high heat.
2. Rinse and quarter potatoes, but do not peel. Place potatoes, together with carrots for carrot recipe, in vegetable steamer, cover, and steam over high heat until barely tender (you should be able to insert fork without resistance), about 10 to 12 minutes. (Water level must not reach steamer.) Remove pan from heat, uncover, and cool slightly.
3. Cut potatoes into ¾-inch cubes.
4. In medium-size saucepan, melt butter over medium heat. Add shallots and sauté until soft and translucent, about 1 minute. Add parsley and thyme. Add potatoes and toss gently until they are warmed through. Season to taste with salt and pepper. Transfer to heatproof serving bowl and keep warm in 200-degree oven until ready to serve.

Victoria Wise

Victoria Wise, a California-based restaurateur and chef, joins classic French cooking techniques with a nonclassic approach to combining flavors and ingredients. A childhood spent in Japan and extensive travel in Europe have given her a broad cultural perspective for her menu planning. Working in California, where cooks have abundant seasonal produce and fresh aromatic herbs year round, has further enhanced her eclectic style.

Her first menu is a perfect example of how her travels have influenced her. She presents a Mediterranean-style flank steak that is first filled with chopped spinach and diced carrots, then rolled up jelly-roll style, and finally soaked in a rich and flavorful marinade of both Oriental and Western ingredients: soy sauce, fresh ginger, and fresh coriander with red wine, olive oil, and a bay leaf.

For Menu 2, Victoria Wise pairs two Italian-inspired dishes—an herbed veal caponata and a creamy Parmesan-sprinkled fettuccine. She serves these with a refreshing salad of tomato and crisp-tender asparagus dressed with a shallot vinaigrette. In Menu 3, Napa, also known as Chinese or celery cabbage, is used to wrap seasoned lean ground meat, making a lighter, exotic version of the Eastern European mainstay, stuffed cabbage.

A roulade of flank steak and spinach creates a pinwheel effect. The perfect companions to this elaborate-looking entrée are cottage fried potatoes seasoned with coriander and a tarragon-scented salad with mushrooms.

Warm Tarragon-Mushroom Salad
Beef Roulade
Cottage Fried Potatoes

Flank steak is a thick, flavorful cut of beef with a pronounced grain that makes it well suited for this roulade. Butterflying this—or other cuts of meat—is not difficult if you have a well-sharpened chef's knife. Simply make a smooth, even cut (with the grain) horizontally through the center of the meat, slicing almost, but not entirely, through the steak so that you leave a ½-inch "hinge" at one edge. Gently open the steak out like a book on a smooth surface and flatten it slightly with a wooden mallet. This will make it easier to roll after you spread the stuffing on the meat.

In the warm, tarragon-scented salad, the cook suggests combining fresh mushrooms with *shiitake*, which are thick, brown Japanese mushrooms with a distinct aroma and flavor. They are available in many specialty food stores and Oriental markets. If you cannot find fresh *shiitake*, substitute the dried variety, which is easily reconstituted by soaking for 15 to 20 minutes in hot water. If you cannot find butter lettuce, use red-leaf lettuce or watercress in the salad.

Fresh coriander, which is used in the roulade and cottage fries recipes, is a pungent herb that looks like parsley but doesn't taste like it. If you find the flavor of coriander too powerful, use fresh thyme or parsley instead.

WHAT TO DRINK

The cook suggests a Napa or Amador County Zinfandel to accompany this menu. A Cotes du Rhône or a Chianti would be good alternatives.

SHOPPING LIST AND STAPLES

1 beef flank steak (about 1¾ pounds trimmed weight), butterflied
5 russet potatoes (about 3 pounds total weight)
⅓ pound shiitake mushrooms, if available
⅔ pound fresh mushrooms, or 1 pound if not using shiitake
1 head butter or red-leaf lettuce
1 to 1½ pounds spinach
Medium-size carrot
2 large lemons
10 cloves garlic
1-inch piece fresh ginger
Medium-size bunch fresh coriander or parsley
Small bunch fresh tarragon, or 1 teaspoon dried

2 tablespoons unsalted butter
½ cup plus 3 tablespoons olive oil
½ cup vegetable shortening or oil
⅔ cup soy sauce
1 loaf French bread (optional)
1 bay leaf
Salt
Freshly ground peppper
2 cups dry red wine

UTENSILS

Food processor (optional)
2 large heavy-gauge non-aluminum skillets, one with ovenproof handle
Medium-size non-aluminum saucepan
Large non-aluminum roasting pan
Small roasting pan
Large platter
Colander or sieve
Salad spinner (optional)
Measuring cups and spoons
Chef's knife
Paring knife
Slotted metal spatula
Wooden spoon
Wooden mallet or rolling pin
Grater
Juicer (optional)
Vegetable peeler
Meat thermometer (optional)
Kitchen string

START-TO-FINISH STEPS

1. Chop fresh tarragon, if using, for mushroom salad and chop coriander or parsley for potatoes.
2. Follow roulade recipe steps 1 through 7.
3. While marinade is reducing and roulade is cooking, follow potatoes recipe steps 1 and 2.
4. Follow mushroom salad recipe steps 1 through 3 and place French bread, if serving, in 350-degree oven to warm.
5. Follow roulade recipe step 8 and potatoes recipe step 3.
6. Follow salad recipe step 4 and serve as first course with French bread.

7. Follow roulade recipe step 9 and potatoes recipe step 4, and serve.

RECIPES

Warm Tarragon-Mushroom Salad

⅓ pound shiitake mushrooms, if available
⅔ pound fresh mushrooms, or 1 pound if not using
   shiitake
6 cloves garlic
1 head butter or red-leaf lettuce
1 large lemon
1 tablespoon chopped fresh tarragon leaves, or 1 teaspoon
   dried
2 tablespoons unsalted butter
3 tablespoons olive oil
Salt
Freshly ground pepper
1 teaspoon chopped fresh tarragon for garnish (optional)
1 loaf French bread (optional)

1. Clean mushrooms with damp paper towels. Using paring knife, trim stem ends and cut each cap into 3 or 4 slices. Set aside.
2. Peel garlic and cut into slivers. Set aside.
3. Wash lettuce and dry in salad spinner or pat dry with paper towels. Divide among 4 salad plates. Set aside.
4. Juice lemon. Strain out pits and reserve juice. In large heavy-gauge non-aluminum skillet, heat butter and oil over high heat. When butter foams, add mushrooms and sauté, stirring with wooden spoon, 3 to 4 minutes. Add garlic, tarragon, and lemon juice, and stir 2 to 3 minutes longer, or until liquid is reduced by one third. Season with salt and pepper to taste and spoon over lettuce-lined plates while still warm. Garnish with chopped fresh tarragon and serve with warm French bread, if desired.

Beef Roulade

1 beef flank steak (about 1¾ pounds trimmed weight),
   butterflied
1-inch piece fresh ginger
4 cloves garlic
½ large lemon
2 cups dry red wine
⅔ cup soy sauce
½ cup olive oil
1 bay leaf
6 sprigs fresh coriander or parsley
1 to 1½ pounds spinach
Medium-size carrot
Salt
Freshly ground pepper

1. Have butcher butterfly flank steak, if possible. Otherwise, carefully do it yourself using sharp chef's knife. Gently open the steak out like a book on smooth surface and, using a wooden mallet or rolling pin, flatten it slightly, being careful not to tear hinges. Set aside.

2. Preheat oven to 475 degrees.
3. Peel and coarsely grate ginger. Peel and coarsely chop garlic. Juice lemon and strain out pits.
4. In large non-aluminum roasting pan, combine ginger, garlic, lemon juice, wine, soy sauce, olive oil, bay leaf, and coriander. Open butterflied steak and place in marinade, cut side down. Set aside 15 minutes.
5. Wash spinach in several changes of cold water. Remove stems and discard. Drain in colander or sieve; do not dry. Cut leaves into ½-inch wide strips. Peel and finely dice carrot. In medium-size non-aluminum saucepan, cook spinach and carrot, stirring with wooden spoon, over medium heat about 2 minutes, or until spinach is wilted. Drain in colander or sieve and press out excess liquid with wooden spoon. Set aside. Wipe pan.
6. Turn steak once in marinade to moisten outside and transfer to cutting surface, cut side up. Reserve marinade. Spread spinach-carrot stuffing over meat to within ½ inch of sides and moisten with 2 tablespoons marinade. Pour remaining marinade into pan used for vegetables and bring to a boil over high heat. Cook until reduced by about half, approximately 30 minutes. Remove bay leaf.
7. While marinade is reducing, roll flank steak up lengthwise (with the grain) and tie the roll at ½-inch intervals, starting in center. Tuck in ends of steak and tie 1 long piece of string lengthwise around the roll. Place in small roasting pan and put in oven. After 10 minutes, reduce temperature to 350 degrees and cook 20 minutes longer. Meat thermometer should register 135 to 138 degrees.
8. Turn off oven and place serving platter on oven rack to warm. Let roulade rest in oven until ready to serve (no longer than 15 minutes).
9. Transfer roulade to center of warmed serving platter and remove string. Reserve meat juices in roasting pan. Using chef's knife, cut roulade into ½-inch-thick slices and arrange on individual plates. Add reserved meat juices to the reduced marinade, skim off surface fat, and season with salt and pepper to taste. Reheat briefly and serve with the roulade.

Cottage Fried Potatoes

5 russet potatoes (about 3 pounds total weight)
½ cup vegetable shortening or oil
Salt
2 tablespoons chopped fresh coriander or parsley

1. Wash potatoes, but do not peel. Using chef's knife, cut into ¼-inch dice or coarsely chop in food processor.
2. In large heavy-gauge non-aluminum skillet, heat shortening over medium heat. When shortening begins to shimmer and has a faint blue haze, add potatoes and cook until golden, about 25 minutes, stirring occasionally with slotted metal spatula.
3. Transfer to paper-towel-lined platter and keep warm in turned-off oven.
4. To serve, season with salt to taste and sprinkle with chopped coriander or parsley. Divide among individual dinner plates.

Asparagus and Tomatoes with Shallot Vinaigrette
Veal Caponata
Fettuccine Oregano

Serve the tomato and shallot-topped asparagus as a first course or as a side dish with this variation of veal scaloppini.

This menu has a distinctly Italian flavor. Victoria Wise's veal scaloppini dish is flavored with capers, white wine, and a touch of tomato paste. She recommends serving it with fettuccine, a flat, broad egg noodle that you can buy fresh in many specialty food shops. Or you can use a dried packaged fettuccine—choose an imported Italian brand or a domestic one made with durum semolina. If you are not using fresh oregano in the fettuccine recipe, use the best-quality dried oregano you can find. The cook recommends dried Greek oregano.

For the asparagus and tomato recipe, use Italian plum tomatoes, also known as egg tomatoes; they have a more intense flavor and lower water content than most commer-cial tomatoes. Most supermarkets stock them. If fresh asparagus are not in season, serve fresh artichokes in their place—but be sure to allow more time for cooking artichokes. The vinaigrette dressing for the vegetables features shallots; if they are not available, you can substitute chopped onion.

WHAT TO DRINK
The acidic elements in this menu call for a well-chilled white wine; choose a dry and flavorful Italian Pinot Grigio or California Sauvignon Blanc, or a French Muscadet to complement these dishes.

SHOPPING LIST AND STAPLES

Eight to twelve ¼-inch-thick slices veal scaloppini, or leg
 round steak (about 1¼ pounds total weight), preferably
 cut across grain from the rop round, pounded thin
1 pound asparagus
4 medium-size ripe tomatoes (about 1 pound total weight)
3 large shallots
1 lemon
Small bunch fresh oregano, or 1 tablespoon dried oregano
Small bunch fresh parsley or chives (if not using fresh
 oregano)
1 to 2 tablespoons unsalted butter
1 pint heavy cream
¼ pound Parmesan cheese
½ cup plus 3 to 4 tablespoons olive oil
¼ cup red wine vinegar
3½-ounce jar capers
1 tablespoon tomato paste
12 ounces fettuccine, preferably fresh
1 loaf French bread (optional)
½ cup flour (approximately)
Salt and freshly ground pepper
1 cup dry white wine

UTENSILS

Food processor or blender (optional)
Large stockpot with cover
1 or, preferably, 2 large heavy-gauge non-aluminum
 skillets
Small saucepan
9-inch pie pan
Small bowl
Colander
Strainer or slotted spoon
Measuring cups and spoons
Chef's knife
Paring knife
Wooden spoon
Metal spatula
Grater (if not using processor)
Juicer (optional)
Tongs
Small whisk
Vegetable peeler (optional)
Kitchen string

START-TO-FINISH STEPS

1. If serving French bread with asparagus, preheat oven
to 350 degrees.
2. Follow asparagus recipe step 1. While water is coming
to a boil, chop fresh oregano or parsley, or snip chives,
juice ½ lemon, and slice remaining ½ lemon for veal recipe.
Grate Parmesan and chop fresh oregano, if using, for
fettuccine recipe.
3. Follow asparagus recipe steps 2 through 9.
4. Follow veal recipe step 1.
5. Follow fettuccine recipe step 1. While water is coming to
a boil, remove bread from oven, if serving, and lower oven
temperature to 200 degrees. Serve asparagus and warm
bread.
6. Follow fettuccine recipe step 2.
7. While fettuccine is cooking, follow veal recipe step 2.
8. Follow fettuccine recipe steps 3 and 4, veal recipe step
3, and serve.

RECIPES

Asparagus and Tomatoes with Shallot Vinaigrette

1 pound asparagus
4 medium-size ripe tomatoes (about 1 pound total weight)
1 loaf French bread (optional)
3 large shallots
½ cup olive oil
¼ cup red wine vinegar
Salt and freshly ground pepper

1. Fill large stockpot with water to within 3 inches of top,
cover, and bring to a boil over high heat.
2. Wash and trim asparagus. If spears are thick, peel
stems. Divide into 2 bundles and tie with kitchen string so
asparagus can be retrieved more easily. Set aside.
3. Drop tomatoes into boiling water, count slowly to 15,
and then, using slotted spoon, transfer them to colander.
Reserve boiling water for asparagus.
4. Carefully lower both asparagus bundles into the boiling
water. When water returns to a boil, cook asparagus 4 to 12
minutes, depending on size of spears. Be careful not to
overcook.
5. If serving French bread, place in 350-degree oven to
warm.

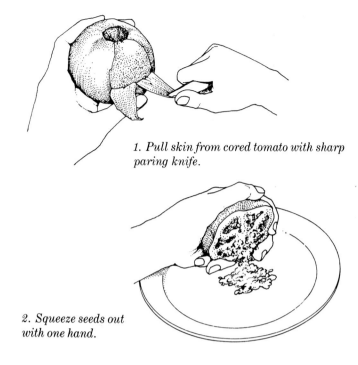

1. Pull skin from cored tomato with sharp paring knife.

2. Squeeze seeds out with one hand.

6. While asparagus are cooking, peel, seed, and dice tomatoes. Drain off juices. Peel and mince shallots.

7. Using tongs, transfer asparagus bundles to colander and rinse briefly in cold water. Reserve boiling water for fettuccine recipe.

8. For dressing, combine tomatoes, shallots, oil, vinegar, and salt and pepper to taste in small bowl.

9. Untie asparagus bundles and divide spears among 4 salad plates. With a fork, stir vinaigrette and pour over asparagus. Cover loosely and set aside until ready to serve.

Veal Caponata

2 tablespoons capers
1 to 2 tablespoons unsalted butter
2 to 3 tablespoons olive oil
Eight to twelve ¼-inch-thick slices veal scaloppini, or leg round steak (about 1¼ pounds total weight), preferably cut across grain from the top round, pounded thin
½ cup flour (approximately)
1 cup dry white wine
Juice of ½ lemon
1 tablespoon tomato paste
1 tablespoon chopped fresh oregano or parsley or freshly snipped chives
½ lemon, thinly sliced

1. If using salt-packed capers, rinse in cold water and pat dry with paper towels. If using capers packed in vinegar, drain. Set aside.

2. In 1 or 2 large heavy-gauge non-aluminum skillets, heat butter and oil (if using 2 skillets, use a total of 2 table-spoons butter and 3 tablespoons oil) over medium-high heat. Warm serving platter under hot water. Put flour in pie pan and dredge each veal slice lightly. Shake off excess. When butter foams, add veal to pan and quickly

sauté about 1 minute per side. While veal is cooking, dry platter. Using metal spatula, transfer veal slices to platter as they are cooked. Keep warm in 200-degree oven.

3. Add white wine and lemon juice to skillet, stirring up any browned bits clinging to bottom. Add tomato paste and capers, whisking until blended. Pour sauce over veal, sprinkle with oregano, and garnish with lemon slices.

Fettuccine Oregano

12 ounces fettuccine, preferably fresh
1½ cups heavy cream
1 tablespoon olive oil
⅔ cup freshly grated Parmesan cheese
3 tablespoons chopped fresh oregano, or 1 tablespoon dried
Salt and freshly ground pepper

1. Add enough fresh hot water to asparagus cooking water to measure 3 quarts and return to a boil over medium-high heat.

2. Add fettuccine to pot and cook 3 to 5 minutes for fresh, 8 to 12 minutes for dried.

3. While fettuccine is cooking, gently heat cream in small saucepan over medium-low heat just until warm.

4. Drain fettuccine in colander and return immediately to pot. Add olive oil and toss to coat well. Add remaining ingredients and toss. Cover until ready to serve.

ADDED TOUCH

Anjou and Comice are two sweet and juicy varieties of pear, both recommended for this classic French dessert. Pears that seem a bit too firm, even underripe, will soften nicely when poached in the sweetened wine.

Warm Pears Poached in Red Wine

½ lemon
3 cups red wine
½ cup granulated sugar
1 stick cinnamon
4 slightly firm pears, preferably Comice or Anjou
1 cup heavy cream
4 sprigs fresh mint

1. Juice lemon half and strain out seeds. In medium-size non-aluminum saucepan, bring wine, sugar, lemon juice, and cinnamon stick to a boil over medium heat.

2. Peel, halve, and core pears. Lower into poaching liquid and cook 15 minutes, turning pear halves frequently. With slotted spoon, transfer pears to large bowl and set aside.

3. Over medium-high heat, reduce poaching liquid by half. This should take about 20 to 30 minutes. Liquid should be thick and syrupy.

4. To serve, briefly reheat pears in wine syrup. Spoon 2 pear halves with some syrup into each of 4 bowls. Pour cream over each and garnish with mint sprig.

Fresh Tomato Soup with Garlic-Basil Croutons
Cabbage Leaves with Beef Stuffing / Sour Cream with Chives and Dill
Parslied Potatoes

Fresh, thick tomato soup starts this meal of stuffed cabbage leaves with a dill-flavored sour cream sauce and new potatoes. You can garnish the soup with croutons or serve them on the side.

Napa cabbage (also know as celery cabbage), which is called for in this menu, is a mild Oriental cousin of green cabbage that comes in small compact, oblong heads of pale green and white leaves. Its flavor is delicate, combining that of cabbage, lettuce, and celery, and it gives off no strong cabbage odor during cooking. For this recipe, blanch the leaves, then cut out a small wedge from the spine of each leaf so that the leaf will roll up easily. Reserve the cut-out wedges, which you will chop and use as a bed for the stuffed leaves. If you cannot find Napa, use green cabbage instead.

The thick, fresh tomato soup can be made any time of the year, as long as fresh, flavorful tomatoes are available. The cook prefers Italian plum, or egg, tomatoes. (See page 90 for diagrams showing how to peel and seed tomatoes.) If fresh basil is out of season, use fresh or dried thyme, chervil, tarragon, or dill.

WHAT TO DRINK

The cook suggests a California Sauvignon Blanc or a hearty Provençal red—a Gigondas, for example, or a shipper's (rather than an estate-bottled) Châteauneuf-du-Pape. In warm weather, try a lightly chilled rosé from Provence or Anjou.

SHOPPING LIST AND STAPLES

1 pound ground round steak
2 pounds red potatoes
4 medium-size onions (about 2 pounds total weight)
4 pounds ripe tomatoes, preferably Italian plum
Medium-size head green cabbage, preferably Napa
4 cloves garlic
Small bunch fresh parsley
1 bunch fresh basil (enough to yield 16 good-size leaves)
Large bunch fresh oregano, or 1½ tablespoons dried
Large bunch fresh chives or small bunch scallions
Small bunch fresh dill, or 1 teaspoon dried
2 sticks unsalted butter
1 pint sour cream
½ cup plus 1 tablespoon olive oil
1½ tablespoons tomato paste
1 large loaf French bread or baguette
¼ teaspoon allspice
1 bay leaf
Salt
Freshly ground pepper

UTENSILS

Food processor or blender
Large stockpot
Large heavy-gauge skillet
Large saucepan with cover
2 large non-aluminum saucepans with covers
Small saucepan
Medium-size bowl
Small bowl
2 large flat plates
Colander
Sieve
2 slotted spoons
Wooden spoon
Measuring cups and spoons
Chef's knife
Paring knife
Bread knife
Wooden spoon

START-TO-FINISH STEPS

1. Chop fresh oregano, if using, for cabbage recipe and chop parsley for potato recipe.
2. Follow cabbage recipe step 1.
3. While cabbage is being blanched, slice bread for soup recipe and follow steps 1 through 3.
4. Follow cabbage recipe steps 2 through 6.
5. Follow potatoes recipe steps 1 and 2.
6. While potatoes and cabbage are cooking, mince chives and fresh dill, if using, and prepare sour cream.
7. Follow soup recipe steps 4 and 5.
8. Follow cabbage recipe step 7 and potatoes recipe step 3.
9. Follow soup recipe step 6 and serve as first course.
10. Follow cabbage recipe step 8 and serve with sour cream sauce and potatoes.

RECIPES

Fresh Tomato Soup with Garlic-Basil Croutons

4 pounds ripe tomatoes, preferably Italian plum
2 medium-size onions (about 1 pound total weight)
½ cup plus 1 tablespoon olive oil
1 bay leaf
1 bunch fresh basil (enough to yield 16 good-size leaves)
4 cloves garlic
Four ½-inch slices from large loaf of French bread, or eight ½-inch slices from baguette
Salt
Freshly ground pepper

1. Peel, seed, and chop tomatoes. Peel and chop onions. In large non-aluminum saucepan, cook tomatoes, onions, 1 tablespoon olive oil, and bay leaf, covered, over medium heat 30 minutes.
2. While vegetables are cooking, wash basil and pat dry with paper towels. Strip leaves from stems and stack them so that they all point in same direction. Slice into strips and set aside.
3. Peel and chop garlic. Set aside.
4. In large heavy-gauge skillet, heat ½ cup olive oil over medium-high heat. Add garlic, stir, then add bread slices. Fry briefly on both sides until golden, about 1 to 2 minutes. Transfer croutons to paper-towel-lined plate.
5. Remove bay leaf from tomato mixture and discard. In food processor or blender, purée tomato mixture in batches, about one quarter of mixture at a time. Pour purée back into pan through a sieve, pressing through with wooden spoon, if necessary. Season with salt and pepper to taste. Cover and keep warm until ready to serve. If necessary, reheat before serving.
6. To serve, divide croutons among 4 bowls, sprinkle bowls with half the basil, fill with soup, and garnish each with remaining basil. Or, if you prefer, garnish soup with basil and serve croutons on the side.

Cabbage Leaves with Beef Stuffing

Medium-size head green cabbage, preferably Napa
2 medium-size onions (about 1 pound total weight)
1 pound ground round steak
4 tablespoons chopped fresh oregano, or 1½ tablespoons dried
¼ teaspoon allspice
1½ tablespoons tomato paste
Salt
Freshly ground pepper
1 stick plus 4 tablespoons butter
Sour Cream with Chives and Dill (see following recipe)

1. Fill large stockpot with water to within 3 inches of rim and bring to a boil over high heat. If using green cabbage,

blanch 15 minutes; if using Napa, blanch 5 minutes. Transfer cabbage to colander and drain.

2. Peel and mince onions. In small saucepan, cover onions with water, bring to a boil, and simmer 5 minutes. Pour through sieve and cool slightly.

3. In medium-size bowl, knead together ground round steak, blanched onions, oregano, allspice, tomato paste, and salt and pepper to taste.

4. One by one, gently peel leaves from cabbage. When you reach the core, reserve it. Using paring knife, trim core wedge from each leaf and reserve. Using chef's knife, roughly chop core and trimmings, and set aside.

5. Divide meat stuffing among cabbage leaves, placing 1 to 2 tablespoons stuffing in center of each leaf, and fold into neat "packages."

6. In large non-aluminum saucepan, melt butter over medium heat. Add chopped cabbage core and trimmings, and lay cabbage "packages" on top, folded side down. Season with salt to taste, cover, and simmer 20 minutes.

7. Remove pan from heat and keep covered until ready to serve.

8. To serve on platter, first remove cabbage rolls to plate and then transfer bed of chopped cabbage to platter. Place "packages" on cabbage bed and surround with parslied potatoes (see following recipe). Dot "packages" with a little sour cream sauce (recipe following) and serve remaining sauce on side.

Sour Cream with Chives and Dill

4 tablespoons minced fresh chives or scallions
1 tablespoon minced fresh dill, or 1 teaspoon dried
1 pint sour cream

In small bowl, combine all ingredients. Cover and set aside until ready to serve.

Parslied Potatoes

2 pounds red potatoes
Salt
4 tablespoons butter
4 tablespoons chopped fresh parsley
Freshly ground pepper

1. Wash but do not peel potatoes. Using chef's knife, cut potatoes in half if small, in quarters if large.

2. Place potatoes in large saucepan with water to cover and 2 teaspoons salt. Bring to a boil and cook, covered, until knife inserted in center of potatoes penetrates easily, about 20 minutes.

3. Drain potatoes in colander. Return them to warm saucepan for 2 or 3 minutes to dry out. Return saucepan to medium heat and add butter. Gently toss potatoes in the melting butter until well coated. Add parsley and salt and pepper to taste. Toss gently, cover, and keep warm until ready to serve.

───────────

ADDED TOUCH

Prepare this refreshing minty lemon ice ahead of time and serve in scooped-out lemon halves garnished with mint sprigs. Freezing the lemon halves helps them to keep their shape and gives them an appealing frosty coat when they are served.

Lemon-Mint Ice

⅔ cup sugar
30 to 35 fresh mint leaves
4 to 5 lemons
1 cup sweet white wine or Champagne
Fresh mint sprigs for garnish

1. In small non-aluminum saucepan, bring sugar and ½ cup water to a boil over medium-high heat without stirring. Remove from heat and add mint leaves. Steep mint 5 minutes.

2. Juice enough lemons to measure ⅔ cup juice. Strain out pits. Cut thin slice of rind from outer curve of each lemon half so halves will sit flat. Using paring knife, remove remaining pulp from halves or, using teaspoon, press pulp flat against inside of rind.

3. Add lemon juice and wine to mint syrup in pan and stir to combine.

4. Strain out mint leaves and pour lemon mixture into ice-cube tray or glass bowl. Place in freezer for about 6 hours, or until frozen. To ensure proper texture, occasionally stir mixture, pushing edges down and in along sides of tray or bowl.

5. Remove lemon-mint ice from freezer 30 minutes before serving time. When softened, scoop ice into reserved lemon halves.

6. Return to freezer briefly, just until ready to serve. Garnish each lemon half with a fresh mint sprig and serve with chocolates, if desired.

Gene Hovis

MENU 1 (Left)
Veal Chops Supreme
Broccoli with Pine Nuts
Popovers

MENU 2
Veal Stroganoff
Buttered Zucchini, Carrots, and Cauliflower

MENU 3
Consommé Royale
Wheat-Germ-Breaded Veal Scallops
Baked Stuffed New Potatoes

Gene Hovis grew up on a North Carolina farm where he and his family produced nearly everything for their dinner table, including the creamy pale veal that has always been one of his favorite meats. Later, in Europe, he discovered a new world of veal dishes, particularly in Italy and France. All the menus here have roots in European cuisines.

The veal chops in the first menu are similar to some chops Gene Hovis first tasted in a small Paris restaurant that specialized in veal. He has added mushrooms and onions, and serves them with sautéed broccoli with pine nuts and hot popovers.

The Veal Stroganoff in Menu 2, which is flavored with vodka and a medley of other seasonings, is a lighter and subtler variation of a Franco-Russian beef dish. It is accompanied by spinach and egg noodles tossed with poppy seeds and parsley, as well as steamed zucchini, carrots, and cauliflower flavored with dry vermouth.

The main course of Menu 3 is an adaptation of an Italian scaloppini Marsala. Because he likes its nutty taste, Gene Hovis coats the thin veal scallops with toasted wheat germ, then quickly browns them. He serves the scallops with a Marsala-cream sauce. They are paired with baked and stuffed new potatoes. These small potatoes cook quickly and are an elegant addition to this meal.

Thick veal chops, mushrooms, and broccoli sprinkled with pine nuts are a special-occasion menu, particularly when accompanied by fresh flowers and a good wine. Popovers are an easy alternative to homemade rolls.

95

Veal Chops Supreme
Broccoli with Pine Nuts
Popovers

The veal loin chop is equivalent to a T-bone or Porterhouse steak. Dusting the chops lightly with flour before sautéing helps them to brown properly. The sauce is quick and easy, based on deglazing (see page 12).

The cook lets the trimmed broccoli stand in ice water before cooking to help it retain firmness and color. Cooking it in chicken stock instead of water adds flavor, and the sautéed pine nuts provide crunchiness.

Gene Hovis uses low-fat milk instead of whole milk in the popovers because he believes it makes them lighter. Preheating the custard cups in the hot oven before pouring in the batter is important because it ensures that the popovers will puff up as high as possible.

WHAT TO DRINK

A red Bordeaux, a Margaux, or a St. Julien from one of the small châteaux would be a fine choice.

SHOPPING LIST AND STAPLES

4 veal loin chops (4 to 5 ounces each), cut ½ to ¾ inch thick
¼ pound thickly sliced smoked bacon
1 bunch broccoli (about 1½ pounds)
16 small white silverskin onions (about 1 to 1½ pounds total weight)
12 medium-size firm mushrooms (about ½ pound total weight)
2 large eggs
1 cup low-fat milk
½ pint heavy cream
2 tablespoons salted butter
½ cup chicken stock, preferably homemade (see page 13), or canned
¼ cup safflower or vegetable oil
2 tablespoons Dijon mustard
1⅓ cups all-purpose flour
1 ounce pine nuts
1 teaspoon kosher salt (optional)
Salt and freshly ground pepper
⅓ cup Cognac or brandy

UTENSILS

Large heavy-gauge skillet
Small skillet
Medium-size saucepan with cover
Shallow baking dish or pie plate
Large platter
Large bowl
Medium-size bowl
8 medium-size custard cups
16 x 11-inch cookie sheet
Colander
Strainer or sieve
Measuring cups and spoons
Chef's knife
Paring knife
Slotted metal spoon
Wooden spoon
Metal spatula
Whisk

START-TO-FINISH STEPS

At least 30 minutes ahead: Bring eggs to room temperature.

1. Follow popovers recipe step 1 and broccoli recipe step 1.
2. Follow popovers recipe steps 2 and 3, and veal recipe steps 1 and 2.
3. Follow popovers recipe steps 4 and 5.
4. While popovers are baking, follow veal recipe steps 3 through 8.
5. While mushrooms are browning, follow broccoli recipe steps 2 and 3.
6. Follow veal recipe steps 9 through 11, broccoli recipe step 4, and serve with popovers.

RECIPES

Veal Chops Supreme

4 veal loin chops (4 to 5 ounces each), cut ½ to ¾ inch thick
16 small white silverskin onions
12 medium-size firm mushrooms (about ½ pound total weight)
¼ pound thickly sliced smoked bacon
⅓ cup all-purpose flour
Salt and freshly ground pepper
⅓ cup Cognac or brandy
2 tablespoons Dijon mustard
1 cup heavy cream

1. Trim chops by removing tail bone and any extra fat.
2. In medium-size saucepan, bring 4 cups water to a boil over high heat. Reduce heat to medium. Add onions, unpeeled, and simmer 10 minutes. While onions are cooking, wipe mushrooms clean with damp paper towels and trim off stems level with cap to help mushrooms brown evenly.
3. Pour onions into colander and refresh under cold running water. Trim off roots and remove skin.
4. Using chef's knife, mince bacon. In large heavy-gauge skillet, cook minced bacon over medium heat until crisp, stirring occasionally with metal spatula. Using slotted spoon, transfer bacon to paper towels, reserving fat in skillet.
5. Place flour in shallow baking dish or pie plate. Lightly salt and pepper veal chops, then dredge lightly in flour.
6. Reheat reserved fat in skillet over medium heat. When fat is hot (not sizzling), add chops, and brown them evenly, about 2 minutes on each side, turning with spatula.
7. Gently move chops to side of pan. Add onions to cleared space in center and brown evenly on all sides, about 8 to 10 minutes, stirring frequently with spatula. Turn chops.
8. Gently move onions to side of skillet. Add mushrooms to center of pan and brown, stirring frequently, about 8 to 10 minutes. Warm platter under hot running water.
9. Transfer chops, onions, and mushrooms to warm platter. Cover loosely and keep warm on top of stove. Warm dinner plates under hot running water.
10. Stirring vigorously with wooden spoon, add Cognac and deglaze skillet, scraping up brown bits from bottom of pan. Whisk in Dijon mustard. Add cream, bacon, and salt and pepper to taste, and stir to combine. Cook over medium heat, stirring constantly, until mixture is hot and slightly thickened, about 3 to 5 minutes. Do not boil.
11. Dry plates. Pour sauce through strainer or sieve into small serving bowl or sauceboat. Spoon some sauce onto each plate and top with a chop and a portion of mushrooms and onions. Serve extra sauce separately.

Broccoli with Pine Nuts

1 bunch broccoli (about 1½ pounds)
½ cup chicken stock
¼ cup safflower or vegetable oil
1 teaspoon kosher salt (optional)
2 tablespoons salted butter
¼ cup pine nuts

1. Rinse broccoli. With chef's knife, trim off stems and cut into flowerets. Reserve stems for another use. Immerse flowerets in large bowl of ice-cold water until ready to proceed.
2. In saucepan used for onions, bring chicken stock to a boil over high heat. Reduce heat to medium. Add broccoli, pour oil evenly over flowerets and sprinkle lightly with kosher salt. Cover and cook 8 to 10 minutes.
3. While broccoli is cooking, heat butter in small skillet over medium heat. Add pine nuts and sauté until golden.
4. In colander, drain broccoli. Divide among individual dinner plates and sprinkle with pine nuts.

Popovers

2 large eggs, at room temperature
1 scant cup all-purpose flour
1½ teaspoons salt
1 cup low-fat milk

1. Preheat oven to 450 degrees.
2. Place eggs in medium-size bowl and, using whisk, beat thoroughly. Add flour, salt, and milk and beat with wooden spoon until well blended. Batter should have consistency of heavy cream.
3. Butter 8 medium-size custard cups and place in oven 4 to 5 minutes.
4. Stir batter thoroughly, making sure to stir from bottom, and pour in 2 batches into measuring cup to make filling the custard cups easier.
5. Fill hot custard cups two thirds full and place on cookie sheet. Bake 25 minutes, then turn down oven to 375 degrees and bake another 20 minutes. Do not open oven door until popovers are ready to be brought to the table.

————

ADDED TOUCH

As a light first course for this menu, these dill-pickled shrimp can be prepared the night or morning before, but at least 1 hour ahead.

Dill-Pickled Shrimp

1 small onion
1 stalk celery
3 tablespoons wine vinegar
4 sprigs parsley
1 tablespoon pickling spices
1 bay leaf
3 whole peppercorns
1 tablespoon salt
1½ pounds medium-size shrimp
1 tablespoon safflower or vegetable oil
3 tablespoons chopped fresh dill
1 head Bibb lettuce
1 lemon cut into wedges

1. Peel and chop onion; trim and chop celery.
2. In medium-size saucepan, bring 4 cups water, vinegar, onion, celery, parsley, pickling spices, bay leaf, peppercorns, and salt to a boil. Boil 10 minutes. Add shrimp and cook just until pink, about 5 minutes (do not overcook).
3. Using large slotted spoon, immediately remove shrimp and drain in colander. Rinse under cold running water. Reserve cooking liquid.
4. Peel and devein shrimp.
5. Strain broth into large bowl and cool. Add peeled and deveined shrimp, oil, and dill. Cover and refrigerate at least 1 hour.
6. Just before serving, separate Bibb lettuce into leaves, wash, and dry in salad spinner or pat dry with paper towels. Line 4 plates with lettuce. Drain shrimp and arrange on lettuce-lined plates. Serve with lemon wedges.

Veal Stroganoff
Buttered Zucchini, Carrots, and Cauliflower

Served on a bed of noodles and accompanied by a colorful vegetable side dish, this veal Stroganoff is ideal for a buffet dinner.

This variation of beef Stroganoff is lower in fat than is beef. Use leg veal, cut in half-inch strips so that the meat will remain moist and tender. Dried mushrooms, available in most supermarkets in half-ounce containers, add a distinct woodsy flavor. The common fresh variety are acceptable, although they do not add the same special taste.

WHAT TO DRINK

Stroganoff goes best with a full-bodied, dry white wine; try a California Chardonnay or a white Burgundy.

SHOPPING LIST AND STAPLES

2 pounds lean veal (from leg round roast), cut into strips
  2 inches long, ½ inch wide, ¼ inch thick
2 small zucchini (about 1 pound total weight)
1 pound carrots
Small head cauliflower (about 1¼ pounds)
Medium-size onion
1 bunch parsley
1 lemon
2 cloves garlic
½ pint sour cream

2 sticks salted butter
6-ounce can tomato paste
½ pound spinach noodles
½ pound plain egg noodles
½ ounce domestic dried mushrooms
½ ounce poppy seeds
¼ cup paprika
Salt and freshly ground pepper
½ cup dry vermouth
½ cup vodka

UTENSILS

2 stockpots
Medium-size Dutch oven
2 medium-size saucepans with tight-fitting covers
2 small saucepans
Large heatproof plate
2 medium-size bowls
2 small bowls
Colander or sieve
Large strainer
Measuring cups and spoons
Chef's knife
Paring knife
Slotted metal spoon
2 wooden spoons
Metal spatula

START-TO-FINISH STEPS

1. Follow Stroganoff recipe step 1.
2. While mushrooms soak, follow zucchini recipe step 1.
3. Follow Stroganoff recipe steps 2 through 9.
4. Follow zucchini recipe step 2 and Stroganoff recipe step 10.
5. Follow zucchini recipe step 3 and Stroganoff recipe step 11.
6. Follow Stroganoff recipe steps 12 and 13 and zucchini recipe step 4.
7. Follow Stroganoff recipe step 14, zucchini recipe step 5, and serve.

RECIPES

Veal Stroganoff

¼ cup domestic dried mushrooms
Medium-size onion
2 cloves garlic
¼ cup paprika
1 teaspoon salt
2 to 3 teaspoons freshly ground pepper
2 pounds lean veal (from leg round roast), cut into strips 2 inches long, ½ inch wide, ¼ inch thick
1 stick plus 4 tablespoons salted butter
6-ounce can tomato paste
½ cup vodka
½ pound spinach noodles
½ pound plain egg noodles

2 tablespoons poppy seeds
¼ cup plus 2 tablespoons chopped parsley
1 tablespoon lemon juice
1 cup sour cream

1. Rinse mushrooms. Place in medium-size bowl with boiling water to cover and soak 15 to 20 minutes.
2. Drain mushrooms in colander or sieve set over another medium-size bowl, reserving 2 cups soaking liquid. Strain liquid over small bowl and set aside. Wipe out both bowls.
3. Finely chop mushrooms, onion, and garlic.
4. On wax paper, mix paprika, salt, and pepper. Dredge veal strips in mixture.
5. Preheat oven to 200 degrees.
6. In Dutch oven, heat 1 stick butter over medium heat until butter turns amber. Add veal in small batches, and brown evenly. Transfer veal to heatproof plate and keep warm in oven until remaining veal is browned.
7. To each of 2 stockpots, add 4 quarts water, cover, and bring to a boil.
8. Add garlic, onion, and mushrooms to Dutch oven and cook over medium heat 5 minutes, stirring occasionally. Add tomato paste and vodka, and stir to combine.
9. Bring mushroom mixture to a boil. Add veal and cook over medium heat 10 to 15 minutes.
10. While veal is cooking, cook noodles, each variety in a separate pot, according to package directions.
11. In small saucepan, melt 4 tablespoons butter.
12. Separately, drain noodles. Turn each into one of the bowls used for mushrooms. Toss each variety of noodle with 2 tablespoons melted butter, 1 tablespoon poppy seeds, and 2 tablespoons chopped parsley.
13. In small bowl, mix lemon juice with sour cream.
14. Remove veal and mushroom mixture from heat. Add sour cream mixture and stir gently to combine. Do not reheat. Pile in center of platter and surround with spinach and egg noodles. Sprinkle with remaining parsley.

Buttered Zucchini, Carrots, and Cauliflower

Small head cauliflower (about 1¼ pounds)
2 small zucchini, cut into ¼-inch-thick rounds
1 pound carrots, peeled and cut diagonally into ½-inch-thick pieces
½ cup dry vermouth
Salt
4 tablespoons salted butter
1 tablespoon chopped parsley

1. Break cauliflower into flowerets and wash thoroughly.
2. In each of 2 medium-size saucepans, bring ½ cup water, ¼ cup vermouth, and salt to taste to a boil.
3. Add carrots and cauliflower to saucepans. Return to a boil and cover both pans tightly. Cook carrots 10 minutes and cauliflower 8 to 10 minutes. Three to 4 minutes before cauliflower is done, add zucchini to saucepan.
4. While vegetables are cooking, melt butter in small saucepan.
5. Drain vegetables in colander. Transfer to serving bowl and toss with melted butter and parsley.

Consommé Royale
Wheat-Germ-Breaded Veal Scallops
Baked Stuffed New Potatoes

Veal scallops, or scaloppini, are thin slices cut from the leg. For this recipe, they should be about a quarter inch thick. If they are not thin enough, put them between sheets of wax paper and pound them with a wooden mallet or rolling pin. Remove any fat or filament before seasoning, breading, and sautéing.

Instead of bread crumbs, the cook coats the scallops in flour and wheat germ for added flavor, texture, and nutrition. He uses plain wheat germ, not one of the flavored varieties available. Dipping the scallops in the seasoned

Breaded in wheat germ, these veal scallops with Marsala sauce have an unusual texture and a nutty taste. The baked new potatoes have been scooped out, mashed with cream and Parmesan cheese, and repacked in their skins.

beaten egg mixture before breading them helps the wheat germ adhere to the meat during cooking. The sauce is made by deglazing the pan with lemon juice, cream, and Marsala.

New potatoes, which are usually boiled or steamed, are baked here, scooped out of their skins, mashed, seasoned, and put back into the skins for browning. Do not use a food processor to mash the potatoes; it will make them soft and mushy.

WHAT TO DRINK

The flavors here are restrained and need a slightly soft, dry red wine. The range of possibilities includes California Pinot Noir, French Moulin à Vent, and Italian Cabernet.

SHOPPING LIST AND STAPLES

Eight ¼-inch-thick veal scallops (about 1¼ pounds
  total weight), pounded ⅛ inch thick
12 medium-size new red potatoes (about 2 pounds
  total weight)
2 medium-size onions
Small bunch celery, with leaves
2 medium-size carrots
Small bunch watercress (optional)
Small bunch parsley
2 lemons
2 large eggs
1 stick plus 4 tablespoons salted butter
1 pint heavy cream
¼ pound Parmesan cheese
Four 10½-ounce cans beef consommé
⅔ cup safflower oil (approximately)
1 tablespoon mayonnaise
12-ounce jar unflavored wheat germ
½ cup flour
1 tablespoon paprika
Salt
Freshly ground pepper
1 cup dry red wine
⅓ cup dry Marsala

UTENSILS

Large enamel or stainless steel stockpot
2 large heavy-gauge skillets
Small saucepan
Two 13 x 9-inch ceramic or glass baking dishes
Two 15 x 12-inch cookie sheets
Heatproof platter
2 medium-size bowls
Small bowl
Salad spinner (optional)
Strainer or sieve
Measuring cups and spoons
Chef's knife
Paring knife
Wooden spoon
Metal spatula
Whisk
Potato ricer (optional)
Melon baller (optional)

START-TO-FINISH STEPS

1. Follow consommé recipe steps 1 and 2.
2. Follow stuffed potatoes recipe steps 1 through 3.
3. Mince parsley, squeeze lemon juice, and wash and dry

watercress, if using, for veal recipe. Follow veal recipe steps 1 through 6.

4. For potatoes recipe, grate Parmesan cheese and follow recipe steps 4 through 7.

5. Follow consommé recipe step 3.

6. Follow potatoes recipe step 8, and serve consommé, step 4.

7. Remove potatoes from oven and lower oven temperature to 200 degrees. Place platter with veal in oven to reheat briefly as you follow veal recipe steps 7 and 8.

8. Follow veal recipe step 9 and serve with potatoes.

RECIPES

Consommé Royale

2 stalks celery, with leaves
2 medium-size carrots
2 medium-size onions
Four 10½-ounce cans beef consommé
1 cup dry red wine
Small bunch parsley
Salt
Freshly ground pepper
1 lemon

1. Wash celery and cut into quarters. Scrub (but do not scrape) carrots and cut into quarters. Peel and quarter onions.

2. In large stockpot, combine celery, carrots, onion, consommé, wine, and parsley. Cover and bring to a boil over high heat. Reduce heat and simmer, uncovered, 45 minutes.

3. Strain over medium-size bowl and add salt and pepper to taste. Discard vegetables. Warm 4 soup bowls under hot water and dry. Slice lemon thinly.

4. Divide consommé among heated bowls and garnish with lemon slices.

Wheat-Germ-Breaded Veal Scallops

2 large eggs
1 tablespoon minced fresh parsley
1 teaspoon salt
1 teaspoon freshly ground pepper
¾ cup unflavored wheat germ
½ cup flour
Eight ¼-inch-thick veal scallops (about 1¼ pounds total weight), pounded ⅛ inch thick
1 stick salted butter
⅓ cup safflower oil
⅓ cup dry Marsala
1 tablespoon lemon juice
1 cup heavy cream
Small bunch watercress for garnish (optional)

1. In baking dish, beat eggs. Add parsley, salt, and pepper, and stir to combine.

2. On cookie sheet, thoroughly combine wheat germ and flour, stirring with fork.

3. Dip each veal scallop in egg mixture, then dredge in wheat germ mixture, coating well on both sides. Arrange in single layer on wax-paper-lined platter. Refrigerate until ready to proceed.

4. Divide butter and oil equally between 2 large skillets and heat over medium heat until mixtures begin to turn an amber color.

5. Turn heat to medium-high. Gently add scallops and cook in batches, 2 at a time, being careful not to crowd pans or let them touch. Brown scallops evenly, about 2 to 3 minutes on each side, turning with spatula.

6. As scallops are done, transfer them to heatproof platter. When all the scallops are done, cover with foil and keep warm on top of stove.

7. Stirring vigorously, add Marsala and deglaze skillets, scraping up brown bits from bottom of pan. Combine contents of both skillets in one. Whisk in lemon juice and cream, and heat to just below boiling point, about 3 to 5 minutes. Do not boil.

8. Warm 4 dinner plates under hot running water and then dry.

9. Strain sauce into small serving bowl or sauceboat and spoon some onto each plate. Divide scallops among plates and garnish with watercress, if desired. Serve extra sauce separately.

Baked Stuffed New Potatoes

12 medium-size new red potatoes (about 2 pounds total weight)
¼ cup safflower oil
4 tablespoons salted butter
¼ cup freshly grated Parmesan cheese
1 tablespoon mayonnaise
1 tablespoon heavy cream
2 to 3 teaspoons freshly ground pepper
Salt
1 tablespoon paprika

1. Preheat oven to 400 degrees.

2. Wash potatoes, dry with paper towels, and rub with safflower oil.

3. Place potatoes in baking dish and bake 30 to 35 minutes, or until tender. Remove potatoes from oven and cool slightly. Raise oven temperature to 450 degrees.

4. In small saucepan, melt butter over medium-low heat.

5. While butter is melting, remove top of each potato, cutting with paring knife about one-third of the way down.

6. Holding one potato at a time in a folded clean towel, carefully scoop out about ⅔ of flesh with small melon baller or teaspoon. Put flesh through ricer or mash in medium-size bowl.

7. In small bowl, mix melted butter, Parmesan, mayonnaise, cream, and pepper and salt to taste. Add mixture to mashed potatoes, and stir to combine. Refill potato shells, carefully mounding the mixture. Sprinkle each potato with paprika.

8. Place stuffed potatoes on lightly greased cookie sheet and bake 10 to 15 minutes, until tops begin to turn golden.

Acknowledgments

Special thanks are due to Tom McDermott, John Francis, and Marlys Bielunski of the National Livestock and Meat Board, 444 N. Michigan Avenue, Chicago, IL, for their assistance in the preparation of this volume.

The editors would also like to thank the following for their courtesy in lending items for photography: *Cover*: platters—Richard Ginori; board, utensils—WMF of America. *frontispiece*: knife—WMF of America; stainless pan—Pottery Barn; cutting board—Kuttner Antiques. *Pages 18–19*: dishes, trays—Katagiri; linens—China Seas, Inc. *Page 22*: flatware—Wallace Silversmiths; dishes—Pottery Barn; mat, napkin—Urban Outfitters. *Page 24*: bowls, utensils—Dean & DeLuca; handpainted cloth—Peter Fasano. *Page 26*: flatware, napkin, dishes—Frank McIntosh at Henri Bendel; paper—Four Hands Bindery. *Pages 28–29*: dishes, glasses, mats, napkins—Conrans; pitcher—Buffalo China, Inc. *Pages 32–33*: coasters, platters—Pottery Barn; napkins—Frank McIntosh at Henri Bendel. *Page 36*: flatware—The Lauffer Company; napkin—Conrans; dishes—Pottery Barn. *Pages 38–39*: utensils, platters—Pottery Barn. *Page 42*: dish—Pierre Deux. *Page 44*: flatware—Wallace Silversmiths; dish, napkin—Pottery Barn; cloth—Pierre Deux. *Pages 46–47*: dishes—The Museum Store of The Museum of Modern Art; paper—Four Hands Bindery. *Page 50*: utensils—Wallace Silversmiths; dishes—Far Eastern Arts, Inc.; vase—The Museum Store of The Museum of Modern Art. *Page 53*: platters—Pottery Barn; cloth—Brunschwig & Fils. *Pages 56–57*: flatware—Wallace Silversmiths; wooden spoons—Dean & DeLuca; dishes, glass, linens—Pierre Deux. *Pages 60–61*: napkins—Williams Sonoma; plate, baskets—Broadway Panhandler; rug—Pottery Barn. *Page 64*: dishes—Dean & DeLuca; napkins—Fabindia. *Pages 66–67*: casserole, platter—Bennington from Dean & DeLuca; board—Royal Copenhagen. *Page 70*: dish—Baccarat; linens—D. Porthault, Inc. *Page 72*: dish—Dean & DeLuca; tiles—Country Floors, Inc. *Pages 74–75*: flatware—The Lauffer Company; dishes—Dan Levy, courtesy of Frank McIntosh at Henri Bendel; mat—Frank McIntosh at Henri Bendel. *Pages 78–79*: dishes, linens—Conrans. *Page 81*: flatware—The Lauffer Company; dishes, linens—Ludwig of Munich. *Pages 84–85*: flatware—Wallace Silversmiths; dishes—Mottahedeh & Co., Inc. *Page 88*: flatware—The Lauffer Company; dishes—Broadway Panhandler; white bowl—Dean & DeLuca; linens—Fabindia. *Page 91*: flatware—The Lauffer Company; platters—Patrick Loughran Ceramics; countertop—Formica® Brand Laminate by Formica Corp. *Pages 94–95*: flatware, dishes, glasses—Royal Copenhagen; countertop—Formica® Brand Laminate by Formica Corp. *Page 98*: utensils—Wallace Silversmiths; cloth—Brunschwig & Fils; platters—Haviland & Co. *Pages 100–101*: flatware—The Lauffer Company; dishes, glass, tray—Pottery Barn; linens—Laura Ashley. *Kitchen equipment courtesy of:* White-Westinghouse, Commercial Aluminum Cookware Co., Robot-Coupe, Caloric, and Hobart Corp.

Illustrations by Ray Skibinski
Production by Giga Communications

Index

*Time-Life Books Inc. offers a wide
range of fine recordings, including
a Big Band series. For subscription
information, call 1-800-621-7026, or
write* TIME-LIFE MUSIC, *Time & Life
Building, Chicago, Illinois 60611.*